Garden Fresh

Member Recipes

Garden Fresh

Member Recipes

Minnetonka, Minnesota

Garden Fresh Member Recipes

Printed in 2005.

All rights reserved. No part of this publication may be reproduced, stored in an electronic retrieval system or transmitted in any form or by any means (electronic, mechanical, photocopying, recording or otherwise) without the prior written permission of the copyright owner.

Tom Carpenter
Creative Director

Michele Teigen
Senior Book Development Coordinator

Zachary Marell
Book Design and Production

Mowers Photography

Mary Lane
Food Stylist

We would like to thank NHGC members for sending their favorite garden recipes as the foundation for *Garden Fresh Member Recipes*.

4 5 6 7 8 9 / 09 08 07 06 05
© 1999 National Home Gardening Club
ISBN 1-58159-052-0

National Home Gardening Club
12301 Whitewater Drive
Minnetonka, MN 55343
www.gardeningclub.com

The National Home Gardening club proudly presents this special cookbook edition which includes the personal favorites of your fellow Members. Each recipe has been screened by a cooking professional and edited for clarity. However, we are not able to kitchen-test these recipes and cannot guarantee their outcome, or your safety in their preparation or consumption. Please be advised that any recipes which require the use of dangerous equipment (such as pressure cookers) or potentially unsafe preparation procedures (such as canning and pickling) should be used with caution and safe, healthy practices.

contents

Introduction 6

Appetizers 7

Sauces, Dips & Salsas 17

Salads 37

Soups 47

Breads 63

Side Dishes 73

Main Dishes 89

Desserts 127

Index 156

Taste your garden's goodness ...
with these Garden Fresh Member Recipes

Both gardening and cooking present their own challenges.

Gardening's biggest challenge is simple: learning about the plants you love—what they like and don't like—and then providing the proper environment and conditions to grow them successfully. With the right ideas and instructions, you will be successful.

In cooking, for many of us, the main challenge seems to be *ideas* ... coming up—week after week—with the recipes and concepts you need to create great-tasting and interesting dishes for the dinner table—even lunch and breakfast and beyond—as well as any entertaining you might be doing. Once again, ideas plus instructions equal success.

Both pastimes meet in one very special place—the kitchen—and what a wonderful combination it is! Fortunately, nobody knows how to bring together gardening and cooking better than NHGC members who present to you, in this color-filled book, their very best garden-fresh recipe ideas.

Every recipe here includes some kind of produce you can grow in your garden and bring to your kitchen. Of course, sometimes you'll get it at the store or a farmer's market, but the idea is still the same:

These are the recipe ideas that will help you fill your menu plan easily, and even get you looking forward to cooking again, utilizing the bounty of the land. And every one of these recipe ideas is special. Each one is a member's favorite—an idea they've been kind enough to fine-tune, write down and share with other members like you.

The recipe gems that follow are true treasures in a couple ways. They take advantage of garden-fresh produce ... and they have been proven time and time again (often over the course of several generations), in kitchens across our great country.

The challenges of gardening—and cooking—are not that difficult, when you have a friend by your side. Your club is helping you be a better gardener—now let fellow members share their cooking ideas. Then it's time to put these *Garden Fresh Member Recipes* to work in your home too.

appetizers

Beef Negamaki Rolls

Beef Negamaki Rolls

8 spears thin asparagus
1 large carrot, cut into ¼-inch strips
2 round steaks, pounded thin; 8 x 6-inches
Cornstarch
1 large avocado, sliced into wedges
¼ lb. Japanese green beans
1-2 tsp. sesame oil

SAUCE:
1 T. sugar
1 T. mirin
1 T. sake
3 T. soy sauce
2 T. water

Parboil vegetables (not avocado) separately in lightly salted water, until just tender (about 30 seconds-1 minute, depending on the vegetable). Drain vegetables immediately; place in ice water bath to stop cooking. Drain. Pat dry; set aside.

Pound out steak and lightly dust with cornstarch. Lay 3-4 strips of each vegetable (one on top of another) along length of beef; roll up tightly. Make sure vegetables go entire length of meat. Roll beef so it goes around vegetables 1 ½-2 times to prevent it from opening. Cut off excess beef or vegetables if necessary, or utilize them in other rolls. Tie rolls securely with kitchen string at approximately 2-inch intervals to hold in place. Repeat process until all beef and vegetables are used up.

Place sauce ingredients in bowl, stirring to combine and dissolve all the sugar. Put 1-2 teaspoons sesame oil in wok; heat until almost smoking. Place rolls in oil. Sauté, turning until nicely browned. Pour sauce over rolls; continue to simmer over medium-high heat until sauce caramelizes and beef is tender, about 5 minutes.

To serve, cut strings and slice beef rolls into 1-inch rounds. Place on serving platter; drizzle sauce over them. Serve hot.

Jill Freedman
Los Angeles, CA

Tuna Delights

2 (7-oz.) cans tuna, drained
½ cup pitted California olives
½ cup mayonnaise
1 T. lemon juice
Optional: ¾ tsp. curry powder
2 T. chopped sunflower seeds
Salt
Pepper
Pumpernickel cocktail bread slices, toasted
Alfalfa sprouts
Tomatoes, sliced

Combine tuna, olives, mayonnaise, lemon juice, curry powder and sunflower seeds. Salt and pepper to taste. Top cocktail slices with alfalfa sprouts; spoon tuna mixture over sprouts. Top appetizers with slices of tomato and additional sunflower seeds and olives.

Vivian Nikanow
Chicago, IL

Onion Rings

4 eggs, beaten

1 cup milk

1 cup beer

4 cups flour

2 tsp. baking powder

Vegetable oil or shortening

4 extra large onions, sliced into rings ½-inch wide

Kosher salt

Mix together eggs, milk and beer. In each of two bowls, mix together 2 cups flour and 1 teaspoon baking powder. Heat shortening in large saucepan. Dip an onion ring into egg mixture; then dip into first bowl of dry mixture. Re-dip onion ring into egg mixture and then into second bowl of dry mixture. Add onion rings to hot oil in small batches. Cook for 3 minutes or until golden brown. Remove from oil; place on paper towels to drain. Salt to taste; serve immediately.

Christine Vann
Laurinburg, NC

Zesty Zucchini Squares

4 ½ cups grated zucchini

1 ½ cups Bisquick

½-1 cup grated Romano cheese

½ cup oil

6 large eggs, slightly beaten

½ cup finely chopped onion

2 T. chopped fresh parsley

1 cup finely chopped pepperoni

Mix all ingredients well. Lightly grease 9 x 13-inch pan. Bake 35-40 minutes at 350 degrees. Let sit 10 minutes before cutting into small squares.

Tina Walker
Pittsburgh, PA

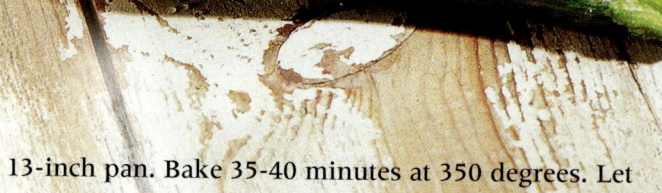

10 appetizers

Potato Puffs

¼ cup milk

1 cup mashed potatoes

1 egg

Salt

Pepper

½ cup grated cheese

Beat milk into mashed potatoes until smooth. Add egg, salt and pepper; stir in grated cheese. Pour into buttered muffin tin. Bake in slow oven for about 15 minutes. Serve hot.

Mary Perkins-Clemons
Bloomington, IN

Scalloped Onions

4 onions, diced

Salt

Water

2 sleeves saltine crackers, crushed

Milk

Boil onions in salt water until tender. Drain. Place in pan; mix with crackers. Add milk until it is visible (the crackers will absorb milk, after the crackers are saturated the milk will then become visible). Bake at 350 degrees until brown on top; 20-30 minutes.

Leslie Hesketh
Waupaca, WI

Shrimp Mousse

Shrimp Mousse

- 1 can tomato soup
- 1 envelope unflavored gelatin
- 8-oz. pkg. cream cheese
- 1 cup mayonnaise
- ½ cup finely chopped onion
- 1 cup finely chopped celery
- 2 small cans shrimp, chopped (or 6 to 8-oz. bag frozen)

Heat soup; add gelatin and cream cheese. Stir until smooth. Remove from heat; cool. Add mayonnaise, onions, celery and shrimp; stir 5 minutes. Grease mold with mayonnaise; pour mixture into mold. Chill until firm. Serve with cocktail crackers.

Note: make the day before needed so mousse has time to set.

Evelyn C. Burandt
Benton Harbor, MI

Mock Crab Cakes

- 2 cups peeled, grated zucchini
- Bread crumbs
- 1 cup Old Bay seasoning
- 1 egg, beaten
- 1 T. oil
- 1 T. butter

Mix together zucchini, bread crumbs, seasoning and egg. Shape into patties. Bread lightly with additional bread crumbs on both sides. Heat oil and butter in skillet. Cook patties until golden brown.

Kurt Garner
Goldsboro, NC

appetizers 13

Savory Herb and Bleu Cheesecake

1 T. butter
⅓ cup dried bread crumbs
2 T. chopped fresh tarragon
9 ½ oz. cream cheese
(1 large block and ½ small block)
6 oz. crumbled bleu cheese
¾ cup sour cream
2 eggs, separated
⅓ cup chopped onion
2 cloves garlic, minced
¼ tsp. pepper
¼ tsp. dry mustard
1 T. oregano
1 T. rosemary
1 T. thyme
1 T. basil

Topping:
1 cup sour cream
1 T. chopped fresh parsley
1 T. chopped fresh chives

Rub sides of 8 or 9-inch springform pan generously with butter. Combine bread crumbs and tarragon; sprinkle crumbs in pan. Swish crumbs around so sides and bottom are coated with crumbs.

Beat cheeses at low speed with electric mixer until well-blended. Add sour cream. Beat for one minute. Add egg yolks, one at a time, beating after each addition. Beat in onion, garlic, pepper, mustard and herbs; set aside. In separate bowl, beat egg whites until stiff peaks form. Fold egg whites into cheese mixture. Pour batter into crumb lined springform pan. Bake at 300 degrees for 1 hour or until set in center.

Combine topping ingredients. When cake is done, remove from oven. Let stand 10 minutes. Spread topping over cake; return to oven for 5 minutes or until sour cream is set. Cool completely before removing from pan. Chill thoroughly. Serve with whole wheat crackers.

Rosemary Johnson
Birmingham, AL

Stuffed-Fried Zucchini Blossoms

3 oz. mild goat cheese, room temperature

1 T. crushed green peppercorns

10-12 zucchini blossoms (with baby zucchini attached)

1 large egg

½ cup tempura batter or flour

Vegetable oil

Mash together goat cheese and peppercorns. Stuff each blossom with approximately 1 tablespoon goat cheese mixture. Dip each blossom into beaten egg, then tempura batter; set aside to dry. Heat oil in skillet until just smoking. Fry zucchini blossoms until golden, turning once. Serve hot.

Jill Freedman
Los Angeles, CA

Frozen Cucumbers

¼ cup pickling salt

4 cups 5% cider vinegar

4 cups sugar

3 qts. thinly sliced cucumbers

2 cups thinly sliced onions

1 bunch celery, thinly sliced

2 red peppers, thinly sliced

2 green peppers, thinly sliced

Mix salt, vinegar and sugar. Pour over vegetables in enamel kettle. Do not heat anything; stir. Put 2 cups vegetables in pint freezer bag. Cover with 1/2 cup syrup. Freeze; will keep in refrigerator one month.

Betty Nelson
Des Moines, IA

Herbed Shallots in Phyllo Purses

2 T. extra virgin olive oil

24 medium shallots, peeled

Kosher salt

Fresh pepper

1 tsp. balsamic vinegar

¼ cup mixed fresh herbs (sage, thyme, oregano, rosemary, parsley, etc.)

3 T. unsalted butter, melted

8 sheets phyllo dough

Heat skillet over moderately-high heat. Add olive oil. Toss shallots with kosher salt and fresh pepper; add to hot oil. Add balsamic vinegar; toss to combine. Cook for 2-3 minutes. Turn down heat to low, cover skillet; simmer for 20 minutes, stirring occasionally until shallots are golden and caramelized. Add herbs, toss to coat; cook 1 more minute. Remove from heat.

Melt butter. Lay out one phyllo sheet on flat work surface. Lightly brush butter onto sheet with pastry brush. Lay next phyllo sheet on top; brush lightly with butter again. Do the same for third and fourth sheets. With sharp knife, cut layered sheets into 6 equal squares. Place two shallots in center of each square. Draw up corners of each square. Firmly pinch together corners leaving top slightly open. This will seal each bundle (they will look like purses). Place each bundle on Teflon coated, ungreased baking sheet. Prepare remaining phyllo sheets in the same manner. Bake at 400 degrees 10-12 minutes until bundles are golden brown all over. Serve hot.

Note: These can be prepared ahead of time and frozen. Will last for weeks in freezer. When ready to serve, preheat oven to 400 degrees, do not thaw bundles. Place frozen bundles in oven and bake until golden, approximately 15-17 minutes.

Jill Freedman
Los Angeles, CA

sauces dips salsas

Southwestern 3 Bean and Corn Salsa

Southwestern 3 Bean and Corn Salsa

2 cups corn
1 red or green bell pepper, seeded, chopped
1 tomato, seeded, chopped
15-oz. can garbanzo beans, drained, rinsed
15-oz. can black beans, drained, rinsed
15-oz. can pinto beans, drained, rinsed
¼ cup sliced green onion
¼ cup balsamic or red wine vinegar
¼ cup olive oil
2 T. finely chopped fresh cilantro or oregano
2 T. chopped fresh parsley
1 T. lemon or lime juice
½ tsp. cumin
¼ tsp. pepper
1 small jalapeño pepper, seed, chopped

Combine all ingredients in large bowl. Chill. Serve with tortilla chips.

Debbie Alquist
Topeka, KS

Corned Beef Dip

8-oz. cream cheese
½ cup sour cream
¼ cup minced green pepper
½ cup minced onion
Dash of garlic powder
2 pkg. corned beef, chopped

Mix cream cheese, sour cream, green pepper, onion and garlic powder. Mix in corned beef. Bake at 350 degrees for 15 minutes. Serve with crackers.

Robin Smilek
Akron, OH

Fire-Roasted Tomato Chipotle Salsa

¼ cup plus 1 T. virgin olive oil

½ onion, peeled, chopped

2 lbs. Roma tomatoes, blackened

4 tsp. finely minced roasted garlic

½ cup minced fresh cilantro leaves

4 chipotle chiles en adobo, chopped

¼ cup red wine vinegar

1 T. salt

1 tsp. sugar

Heat 1 tablespoon olive oil in sauté pan over medium heat until lightly smoking. Add onion; sauté until caramelized. Transfer onion, half the blackened tomatoes and garlic to food processor. Pulse until finely chopped. Add cilantro and chipotle chiles; pulse again to mix. Peel, seed and chop the remaining pound of tomatoes; fold together with remaining ¼ cup olive oil, vinegar, salt and sugar.

Lisa Fritze
Hastings, MN

sauces 19

Lake Charles Dip

½ pint sour cream
1 pkg. dry Italian salad dressing mix
1 T. mayonnaise
Juice of ½ lemon
½ avocado, finely chopped
½ tomato, finely chopped
Dash of Tabasco sauce

Mix all ingredients. Serve in bell pepper cups. Use as dip for assorted vegetables.

Holly Mitchell
Garland, TX

Vegetable Herb Marinade

1 medium red onion, chopped
½ cup dry white wine
¼ cup white wine vinegar
2 cloves garlic
½ tsp. ground pepper
2 T. olive oil
1 T. lemon juice
1 tsp. dried rosemary
1 tsp. dried thyme
1 tsp. freshly grated lemon peel
1 tsp. honey
Fresh vegetables

Place all ingredients except fresh vegetables, in food processor; mix until onion is pureed. Place fresh vegetables in marinade for several hours.

Rita Schaier
Allison Park, PA

Lake Charles Dip

Northport Picante

2-3 large, fresh tomatoes, chopped
½ green pepper, chopped
½ cup thinly sliced scallions
¼ cup fresh parsley
½ tsp. fresh cilantro
2 jalapeño peppers
2 T. peanut/canola oil
½ tsp. sugar
¼ tsp. Tabasco sauce
⅛ tsp. cayenne pepper
⅛ tsp. ground white pepper
⅛ tsp. ground black pepper

Combine ingredients in food processor. Let stand at room temperature for 30 minutes or refrigerate.

Shelly Rine
North Port, FL

Taco Dip

1 lb. hamburger
1 pkg. taco seasoning
8-oz. sour cream
8-oz. cream cheese
12-oz. pkg. shredded cheddar cheese
Tomatoes, chopped
Green pepper, chopped

Brown hamburger; drain. Add taco seasoning (reserve 1/2 teaspoon of mix); prepare per package directions. Blend together sour cream, cream cheese and cheddar cheese, plus 1/2 teaspoon reserved taco seasoning. Spread in bottom of 13 x 9-inch pan. Place hamburger mixture on top of cheese mixture. Layer tomatoes and green pepper over hamburger. Chill; serve with tortilla chips.

Mrs. Sue Grady
Capon Bridge, WV

Hot Artichoke Dip

28-oz. can artichoke hearts, drained, diced
1 1/2 cups grated Parmesan cheese
1 cup mayonnaise
1 cup sour cream
1 T. Tabasco sauce

Mix all ingredients. Bake at 325 degrees for 45 minutes. Serve with tortilla chips.

Irene Gaige
Battle Mountain, NV

Parsley Pesto

Parsley Pesto

2 cups firmly packed fresh parsley
1 T. dried sweet basil
¾ cup grated Parmesan cheese
⅓ cup pine nuts
3 large cloves garlic
½ cup olive oil
½ tsp. freshly ground black pepper

Blend all ingredients in food processor until desired consistency.

Margaret Simon
Nikiski, AK

Curry Dip

½ cup mayonnaise
½ cup sour cream
1 T. fresh lemon juice
½ tsp. curry powder
¼ tsp. salt
Dash of garlic salt
Optional: 2 drops yellow food coloring

Combine all ingredients. Refrigerate; serve with assorted vegetables.

Jean Fields
Apple Valley, CA

Green Tomato Pickles

¼ cup pickling salt

1 qt. water

4 quarts sliced green tomatoes

3 medium onions, sliced

2 cups vinegar

4 cups brown sugar

½ tsp. ground allspice

Mix together pickling salt and water. Pour over tomatoes and onions. Let sit 30 minutes. Drain; rinse. Pour vinegar, brown sugar and allspice over tomatoes and onions. In sauce pan, cook until tender. Seal while hot in sterilized pint jars. Process 10-15 minutes.

Mrs. Willie Grenier
Albion, ME

Spicy Hot Green Tomato Preserves

1 bunch celery, sliced

4-6 large yellow onions, chopped

2 cups olive oil

2 cups wine or apple cider vinegar

1 bulb garlic, minced

1 cup crushed red pepper flakes

Green tomatoes, chopped

Mix all ingredients in large saucepan. Heat mixture until ready to boil. Fill Mason jars. Refrigerate until ready to use. Spread on Italian bread instead of butter or bake with meat (such as pork tenderloin).

Gerald Yunker
Groveland, MA

Zucchini Strawberry Jam

6 cups grated zucchini
6 cups white sugar
Juice of ½ lemon
10-oz. strawberries
6-oz. pkg. strawberry Jell-O

Boil zucchini in large pan for 10 minutes. Add sugar, lemon juice and strawberries. Boil 6 minutes. Add Jell-O, turn off heat; stir until dissolved. Cool; place in jars and freeze. Makes 4-5 pints.

Eldora Merola
Wilton, CA

Spaghetti Sauce

20 cups tomatoes, peeled
3 ½ cups chopped onion
1 green pepper, chopped
4 celery stalks, chopped
8 (6-oz.) cans tomato paste
5 cups water
1 T. pepper
½ T. ground oregano
1 T. garlic powder
3 T. salt
½ cup sugar
5 to 6 bay leaves

Combine all ingredients together in saucepan. Cook for 2 hours, uncovered. Stir frequently. Remove bay leaves; pour sauce into hot jars. Process pints in boiling water bath for 15 minutes. Makes 12-14 pints.

Mrs. Vickie A. Reich
Frederick, SD

Gourmet Mint Butter

1 cup creamery butter, softened

½ tsp. lemon juice

1 cup finely chopped mint

1 tsp. pureed jalapeño peppers

Blend all ingredients. Store in airtight container in cool place.

Susan Ann Olson
Garden Valley, ID

Zucchini Squash Relish

5 T. salt

Water

12 cups ground squash

4 cups chopped onion

4 bell peppers, chopped

4 ½ cups sugar

2 ½ cups vinegar

1 T. black pepper

2 T. celery seed

1 T. dry mustard

1 tsp. nutmeg

1 tsp. turmeric

Mix salt with water. Cover squash, onion, and peppers with solution. Let stand overnight. Drain; rinse with fresh water. Drain again. Place in saucepan. Add sugar, vinegar, pepper, celery seed, mustard, nutmeg and turmeric. Bring to a boil. Cook 35 minutes. If juicy, dip off juice and add 2 to 3 tablespoons cornstarch. Add cornstarched juice back to saucepan the last 5 minutes. Freeze or can in pint size containers.

Sharon Blankenship
Midwest City, OK

Hot Pepper Butter

42 hot peppers

1 pint yellow mustard

1 qt. vinegar

6 cups sugar

1 T. salt

1 cup flour

1 ½ cups water

Grind peppers; place in saucepan. Add mustard, vinegar, sugar and salt; boil. In separate bowl, combine flour and water to make paste. Add to boiling mixture; cook for 5 minutes. Pour into pint jars and seal. Makes 7 pints.

Janet Moore
Cardington, OH

sauces

Pickled Homegrown Garlic, Beans or Asparagus

BRINE:
1 1/2 cups vinegar (5% acidity)
1 1/2 cups water
1/4 cup pickling salt

SEASONING PER 1/2 PINT JAR:
1/4 tsp. dill
1/4 tsp. cayenne pepper
1/2 tsp. sugar
1/8 tsp. garlic salt
1/4 tsp. celery seed

Sterilize jars, lids and caps. In saucepan, boil vinegar, water and pickling salt. Place dill, cayenne pepper, sugar, garlic salt and celery seed in 1/2 pint canning jars. Place vegetable of choice (garlic cloves, beans or asparagus) in jars. If using garlic cloves, omit 1/8 tsp. garlic salt per jar. Pour boiling brine in jar until brine level reaches 1/2 inch below top of jar. Process for 15 minutes. Makes 2 1/2 pints.

Toni E. Keel
Florence, MT

Tabbouleh

2 cups chopped fresh parsley
2 tomatoes, chopped
5-6 scallions, chopped
2 cups prepared bulgur
2 cloves garlic, minced
Juice of 2 lemons
1/4 cup olive oil

Combine all ingredients. Mix thoroughly; chill. Serve with pita bread.

Michelle Jester
Parma, OH

Pickled Homegrown Garlic, Beans or Asparagus

Marvelous Cole Slaw Dressing

Sugar
Oil
Vinegar
Water

Mix equal parts of all ingredients. Add favorite herbs. Salt and pepper to taste.

Janet A. Scibek
Raceland, LA

Salad Dressing

12 red peppers
12 green peppers
12 green tomatoes
1 bunch celery
2 onions
3 ½ cups sugar
2 T. salt
1 tsp. celery seed
1 pint vinegar
1 jar mustard
1 cup flour
1 qt. mayonnaise

Grind together peppers, tomatoes, celery and onions. Mix together sugar, salt, celery seed, vinegar, mustard and flour. Add pepper mixture to sugar mixture; boil. Add mayonnaise. Can and seal.

Mrs. R Babione
Freemont, OH

Parmesan-Green Peppercorn Dressing

1 cup nonfat buttermilk
¼ cup grated Parmesan cheese
¼ cup nonfat sour cream alternative
¼ cup reduced calorie mayonnaise
2 T. lemon juice
2 tsp. crushed, dried green peppercorns
¼ tsp. freshly cracked black pepper
⅛ tsp. salt

Combine all ingredients with wire whisk. Cover; chill.

Kerrie Ann Skuran
Schaumburg, IL

Herb Salt

5 tsp. onion powder
1 T. garlic powder
1 T. paprika
1 T. dry mustard
1 tsp. thyme
1 tsp. basil
½ tsp. pepper
½ tsp. celery seed
1 tsp. dillweed
1 T. dried parsley

Combine all ingredients. Use on fish, chicken and pork.

Evangelin Duenow
Savage, MN

Creamy Cucumber Dressing

1 cup plain low fat yogurt

⅓ cup peeled, seeded, finely chopped cucumber

¼ cup reduced calorie mayonnaise

2 T. chopped green onion

2 T. lemon juice

¼ tsp. salt

¼ tsp. dried whole dillweed

¼ tsp. pepper

Combine all ingredients; stir well. Cover; chill.

Kerrie Ann Skuran
Schaumburg, IL

Hummus

15-oz. can garbanzo beans, drained (reserve ¼ cup juice)
2 cloves garlic, minced
2 T. olive oil
¼ cup tahini
Juice of 1 lemon

Process first four ingredients in blender. Add reserved juice from garbanzo beans and lemon juice to blender. Puree until smooth. Place in airtight container. Chill. Serve with drizzled olive oil and dash of paprika with plenty of pita bread.

Michelle Jester
Parma, OH

White Clam Sauce

2 cloves garlic, finely chopped
¼ cup olive oil
2 (6½-oz.) cans chopped clams, drained, reserve liquid
8-oz. bottle clam juice
1 T. chopped parsley
¼ tsp. basil leaves
Dash of pepper
Parmesan cheese

Sauté garlic in oil until tender. Add reserved clam liquid and remaining ingredients except clams. Heat to boiling. Reduce heat; simmer 5 minutes. Add clams; heat through. Serve over hot cooked pasta. Season with grated Parmesan cheese.

Dorothy Raimondi
Anderson, SC

Kerrie Ann's 1000 Island Dressing

1 1/2 cups mayonnaise
2 eggs, hard-cooked, shredded
1 tsp. grated onion
1 tsp. sweet pickle relish
1 tsp. pepper sauce

1 tsp. dry mustard
1/2 cup chili sauce
1/8 tsp. garlic powder
Salt
Freshly ground pepper

Combine all ingredients; chill.

Kerrie Ann Skuran
Schaumburg, IL

Squash Dressing

2 cups mashed, cooked squash
1 small onion, chopped
2 cups bread crumbs
1 can cream of mushroom soup
1 stick margarine, melted
Pepper

Combine all ingredients. Mix; pour into 1 1/2 quart casserole dish. Bake at 375 degrees for 30-40 minutes.

Sherry Tucker
Lafayette, TN

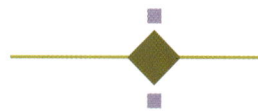

salads

Elegant Beet Salad

Elegant Beet Salad

6 medium beets

2 small shallots, thinly sliced

2 oz. lite olive oil

2 oz. vegetable oil

6 oz. red wine vinegar

1 ½ T. chopped fresh ginger

4 slices canned pineapple, diced

3 celery stalks, cut into thin slices

¾ tsp. salt

½ tsp. freshly ground pepper

Cover beets in cold water; cook for 45 minutes, or until fork tender. Rinse in cold water; let cool. Slip off skin; slice into 1/8-inch slices. Add all other ingredients; toss. Serve on bed of chopped iceberg lettuce at room temperature.

Marianne Petersen
Purcellville, VA

Tri-Pasta Salad

½ box tri-colored pasta, cooked

2-3 ripe tomatoes, chopped

1 bunch fresh broccoli, chopped

1 large red onion, chopped

1 small bottle Italian dressing

1 cup Parmesan cheese

Let pasta cool; place in large bowl. Combine vegetables, dressing, cheese and pasta. Toss until well-coated.

Susan Swearengin
Amelia, VA

German Potato Salad

6-10 large potatoes, chopped
¾ cup chopped onion
6 slices bacon, fried, drained, drippings reserved
2 T. flour
2 T. sugar
2 tsp. salt
½ tsp. celery seed
Dash of pepper
¾ cup water
⅓ cup white vinegar

Boil potatoes; drain. Put in bowl; set aside. Cook onion in bacon drippings until golden brown. Add all dry seasonings; cook until bubbly. Remove skillet from heat; add water and vinegar. Stir until smooth. Put skillet back on heat until mixture boils for 1 minute. Crumble bacon over potatoes. Pour sauce over bacon and potatoes. Stir; serve.

Tina Shook
Sharpsburg, MD

Red and White Salad

1 head cauliflower, chopped
1 cup sliced radishes
½ cup chopped green onion
1 can sliced chestnuts, drained
¾ cup sour cream
¾ cup mayonnaise
Small envelope dry ranch dressing

Combine all ingredients. Chill and serve.

L. Niebruegge
O'Fallon, IL

salads

Avocado and Tomato Salad with Basil Vinaigrette

Avocado and Tomato Salad with Basil Vinaigrette

BASIL VINAIGRETTE:
1/3 cup red wine vinegar
2/3 cup olive oil
3 small garlic cloves, minced
1/3 cup whole fresh basil leaves
1 T. minced fresh parsley
1 T. Dijon mustard
1 tsp. salt
1/8 tsp. freshly ground pepper

SALAD:
2 avocados, quartered lengthwise
2 medium tomatoes, sliced

In medium bowl, combine vinaigrette ingredients. Whisk together, cover and chill. Place tomatoes and avocados on plate, alternating tomato slice and two slices avocado. Place any remaining tomatoes or avocados in center. When ready to serve, whisk vinaigrette then pour over salad.

Lyn Ortiz
Missouri City, TX

Cowboy Salad

3 ½ cups diced fresh tomatoes

4-oz. can chopped green chile peppers

½ medium onion, chopped

1 T. vinegar

1 T. sugar

½ tsp. salt

¼ tsp. pepper

Combine all ingredients. Stir to dissolve sugar and salt. Let set at least 4 hours. It will get hotter the longer it stands. Makes a quart of salad that will keep for several days.

Edgar and Marjorie Evans
Irvine, CA

Jani's Summer Salad

SALAD:

Bibb lettuce

Red onion, thinly sliced

Mandarin orange segments

Kiwi, peeled, sliced

Strawberries, sliced

SALAD DRESSING:

¼ cup sugar

4 T. white vinegar

½ cup light olive oil

Salt

Pepper

Combine dressing ingredients in salad cruet; shake until dissolved. Mix salad ingredients in bowl. Add salad dressing, toss; serve.

Jody Thomae
Ashland, OH

Garden Macaroni Salad

8-oz. pkg. macaroni
1 cup chopped cucumber
1 cup chopped celery
¼ cup chopped green pepper
¼ cup sliced radishes
2 tsp. chopped onion
2 medium tomatoes, chopped
¾ cup mayonnaise
¼ tsp. dried basil

Cook macaroni; drain. Combine with next 6 ingredients, tossing well. Add mayonnaise and basil. Mix well; chill.

Barb Wanzer
Sioux City, IA

Marinated Carrot Salad

2 lbs. carrots, sliced
1 medium onion, chopped
1 medium green bell pepper, chopped
10 ¾-oz. can tomato soup
1 cup sugar
1 tsp. salt
¼ tsp. dill
½ cup corn oil
¾ cup white vinegar
½ tsp. pepper

Cook carrots until slightly tender; drain. Salt lightly; cool. Add onion and green pepper. In separate saucepan, combine tomato soup, sugar, salt, dill, corn oil, vinegar and pepper. Bring to a boil to dissolve sugar. Remove from heat. Pour over vegetables; marinate several hours in refrigerator.

Lucia Smit
Irvine, CA

Southwestern Caesar Salad

1 large clove garlic, split

12 cups mixed greens, torn into bite-size pieces

½ ripe avocado, peeled, diced

1 hot chili pepper

1 cup cilantro leaves

½ cup oil

2 ½ T. fresh lemon juice

2 T. sour cream

1 T. white wine vinegar

1 tsp. Dijon mustard

Salt

Freshly cracked black pepper

3 oz. ranchero cheese, grated

Rub large salad bowl with side of garlic. Add greens and avocado. Mince hot pepper in food processor. Add cilantro; mince. Add oil, lemon juice, sour cream, vinegar, mustard, salt and pepper; mix well. Add dressing to salad. Toss. Sprinkle cheese on top.

Kerrie Ann Skuran
Schaumburg, IL

Broccoli Salad

½ lb. bacon, fried, crumbled
4 cups chopped fresh broccoli
¼ cup chopped green onion
2 cups shredded mozzarella cheese
1 cup mayonnaise
¾ cup sugar
2 T. vinegar

Combine bacon with broccoli, onion and cheese. In separate bowl combine mayonnaise, sugar and vinegar. Pour over broccoli mixture; mix well.

Evelyn Bock
Omaha, NE

Mozzarella and Tomato Salad

1 cup Italian salad dressing
1 T. minced garlic
1 T. balsamic vinegar
1 tsp. dried oregano
1 lb. cherry tomatoes, halved
½ red onion, sliced
12 oz. fresh mozzarella, cubed
6-8 cups spinach
Salt
Pepper

Whisk together salad dressing, garlic, vinegar and oregano. Add tomatoes, onion and mozzarella. Let marinate one hour at room temperature, tossing occasionally. Toss with spinach. Season with salt and pepper.

Jody Thomae
Ashland, OH

Summer Pasta Salad

4-6 oz. rotini or spiral pasta
4 tsp. olive oil
1 tsp. oregano
1 tsp. seasoned salt
¼ tsp. freshly ground pepper
¼ cup minced fresh basil or parsley
1 medium red onion, chopped fine
1 medium cucumber, peeled, seeded, chopped
1 large tomato, cored, seeded, cut into ½-inch cubes

Cook pasta, al dente. Drain; rinse pasta under cool water. Add oil, oregano, salt, pepper, basil and chopped vegetables to cooked pasta. Toss salad; refrigerate for 1 hour prior to serving.

Michelle Cornell
Ann Arbor, MI

soups

Lemon Celery Soup

Lemon Celery Soup

4 potatoes, peeled, sliced
8 stalks celery, sliced
4 to 6 green onions, sliced
3 T. butter
2 (10 ¾-oz.) cans chicken broth
1 can water
3 T. lemon juice
Ground black pepper
Seasoned salt
6 to 8 spinach leaves, stemmed, coarsely chopped
Slivers of lemon rind

Combine potatoes, celery and onions. In medium pan, heat butter. Add vegetables; sauté for 2-3 minutes. Pour in broth, water and lemon juice; boil. Cover; simmer for 15-20 minutes. Puree in food processor. Return to pan; stir in seasonings to taste. Add spinach; heat until spinach is limp. Garnish with slivers of lemon rind. Serve with Parmesan cheese toast.

Sheila Kottke
Torrance, CA

Chicken Tortilla Soup

3 chicken breasts, boneless, skinless
2 cloves fresh garlic, minced
3 cans vegetable broth
1 can water
1 can kernel corn
2 zucchini, sliced
½ red onion, sliced
Cilantro
2 serrano chiles
Cheese, grated

In large skillet, cook chicken and garlic in olive oil. Mix remaining ingredients in saucepan; boil. Reduce to simmer. Cut chicken into strips; add to saucepan. Serve with crushed tortilla chips; top with grated cheese.

Melissa Elam
Simi Valley, CA

Italy's Peasant-Style Tomato Bread Soup

8 oz. Italian country-style bread

¾ cup extra virgin olive oil

1 small yellow onion, finely chopped

¼ cup chopped, fresh sage leaves

3 cloves garlic, pressed

Salt

Pepper

4 cups chicken broth

4 cups beef broth

2 lbs. tomatoes, peeled

Optional: ¼ cup dry white wine

GARNISH:

Olive oil

Parmesan cheese

Cut bread into 1-inch cubes; place on tray for 24 hours to get stale. The next day, heat olive oil over moderate heat in 6-8 quart saucepan. Add onion and sage. Add garlic when onion begins to turn golden on edges. When garlic starts to turn lightly golden, add bread cubes, salt and pepper. Sauté until bread is toasting and turning golden. While bread is toasting, place chicken broth and beef broth into another saucepan; boil. Put tomatoes through food processor; finely chop. When bread cubes are golden, add wine. When bread soaks up wine, add tomatoes; sauté over high heat for 4-5 minutes, stirring and pressing on them to crush further. Pour boiling broth into tomato/bread mixture. Reduce heat, cover; simmer for 40 minutes. Add salt and pepper to taste. Stir occasionally. To serve, drizzle olive oil; sprinkle Parmesan cheese on top.

Jill Freedman
Los Angeles, CA

Potato Leek Soup

6 potatoes, peeled, chopped
2 leeks, chopped
2 onions, chopped
1 carrot, pared, sliced
1 stalk celery, sliced
4 chicken bouillon cubes
1 T. parsley flakes
5 cups water
1 T. salt
Pepper
1/3 cup margarine
1 can evaporated milk

Place all ingredients except evaporated milk, in slow-cooker. Cover; cook on low 10-12 hours. Add evaporated milk just before serving. Serve with chopped chives if desired.

Jean Fields
Apple Valley, CA

Quick New England Chowder

4 strips bacon
1 small onion, chopped
1 stalk celery, diced
2 cups diced potato
1/4 cup diced carrot
1 T. chopped parsley

4-5 cups milk
7 1/2-oz. can minced clams
8-oz. bottle clam juice
Salt
Pepper
Parmesan cheese

Fry, drain and crumble bacon. Sauté onion and celery in bacon fat. Add potatoes, carrots and parsley. Cover with milk and simmer 20 minutes. Add undrained clams, bottled juice and bacon. Cook 2 minutes. Salt and pepper to taste. Serve with grated cheese. Thicken with flour/water if desired.

Note: For richer chowder use half and half instead of milk.

Kathie L. Hoyt
Ancram, NY

Zucchini Soup

3 cups unpeeled, diced zucchini
2-4 strips bacon, slightly cooked, chopped
2 cups chicken stock
1 onion, chopped
1 clove garlic, chopped
2 T. chopped parsley
¼ tsp. salt
Dash of pepper
Sour cream

Combine all ingredients except sour cream. Cook until tender. Put in blender; blend until liquefied. Serve hot or cold. Garnish with sour cream.

Connie Snell
Grand Rapids, MI

Split Pea Soup

6 cups water
⅞ cup split peas
1 T. olive oil
1 carrot, shredded
1 medium onion, chopped
2 cloves garlic, chopped or pressed
1 heaping T. dried parsley
1 tsp. kelp powder
2 bay leaves
½ tsp. salt
1 stalk celery, sliced

Place water, peas and oil in saucepan; boil. Reduce heat; simmer. Add remaining ingredients. Simmer 30-40 minutes until peas are soft.

William A. Pilhofer
Canyonville, OR

Chile-Cheese Chicken Soup with Rice

Chile-Cheese Chicken Soup with Rice

4 slices bacon, fried, drained, crumbled

1 medium onion, chopped

3 cloves garlic, minced

½-1 jalapeño pepper, minced

1 tsp. dried oregano

½ tsp. cumin

⅔ cup rice

½ cup dry white wine

15-oz. can Mexican-style stewed tomatoes

6 cups chicken broth

3 chicken breast halves, skinless, boneless, chopped

Salt

Pepper

4-oz. shredded Monterey Jack cheese

Optional: 2 T. chopped, fresh cilantro or parsley

Leave 2 tablespoons bacon fat in pan. Add onion, garlic and jalapeños. Cook 3-5 minutes. Add oregano, cumin and rice. Cook, stirring for 1 minute. Pour in wine, tomatoes and chicken broth. Reduce heat to medium-low, cover; simmer 30 minutes. Add chicken; simmer 10 more minutes. Season with salt and pepper. Sprinkle shredded cheese, bacon and cilantro/parsley on top.

Mrs. Loine H. Van Pelt
Kernville, CA

Hail Hail for Kale Soup

2 tsp. chopped garlic

1 medium onion, peeled, chopped

2 cups shredded fresh kale (stalks removed)

2 T. canola oil

2 cups chicken broth or stock

16-oz. can whole, peeled tomatoes, diced

8-oz. can tomato sauce

16-oz. can chickpeas, drained, rinsed

½ cup small pasta, uncooked

Desired seasonings (salt, pepper, cayenne pepper, dried tarragon)

Sauté garlic, onion, and kale in oil until kale is slightly cooked; about 5 minutes. Set aside. In soup pot, bring chicken broth to a boil. Add tomatoes, tomato sauce and chickpeas. Simmer 20 minutes. Add kale to mixture. Simmer 30 minutes more. Remove ½ of mixture; puree in blender a little at a time. Return to the soup pot; mix well. Add pasta and seasonings to soup. Simmer 5 minutes.

Nancy Bloomquist
Belfast, ME

Caldo Verde

1 large yellow onion, peeled, minced

1 large clove garlic, peeled, minced

4 T. olive oil

6 large potatoes, peeled, sliced

2 qts. cold water

6 oz. Portuguese chourico, chorizo or pepperoni

2 ½ tsp. salt

¼ tsp. freshly ground black pepper

1 lb. collards, kale or turnip greens, trimmed, thinly sliced

Sauté onion and garlic in 3 tablespoons oil for 2-3 minutes; do not brown. Add potatoes; sauté, stirring constantly 2-3 minutes. Add water, cover; boil 20-25 minutes until potatoes are mushy. Fry sausage in medium skillet over low heat 10-12 minutes, drain well; reserve. When potatoes are soft, remove pan from stove; mash potatoes right in pan. Add sausage, salt and pepper. Return to moderate heat. Cover; simmer 5 minutes. Add collards; simmer uncovered 5 minutes until tender. Mix in remaining tablespoon olive oil, salt and pepper. Serve with Portuguese bread.

Rachel Solveira
Bridgeport, CT

Cody's Soup

1 lb. ground beef

1 medium onion, diced

½ bell pepper, diced

2-3 stalks celery, sliced

1 small can V8 juice

1 can stewed tomatoes

1 can chili beans

2 qts. water

Garlic salt

Black pepper

3-4 medium potatoes, cubed

1 can mixed vegetables

Brown ground beef with onions, green pepper and celery; drain. In large soup pan add ground beef mixture, V8 juice, tomatoes and beans. Simmer 15 minutes. Add 1 quart water, seasonings and potatoes. Cook until potatoes are tender. Add mixed vegetables and as much of remaining 1 quart of water you want. Simmer 15 minutes.

Ms. Betty Davis
Vicksburg, MS

Garden Minestrone Soup

½ cup chopped onion

1 celery stalk, chopped

1 medium zucchini, diced

1 carrot, peeled, diced

10 oz. mushrooms, sliced

1 T. minced garlic

2 tsp. olive oil

3 large tomatoes

3-oz. tomato paste

3 cans vegetable broth

1 tsp. pepper

2 cups cooked small shell pasta

1 can chickpeas

1 can kidney beans

1 can green beans

2 T. chopped fresh basil

1 cup chopped cabbage

In large saucepan, sauté onion, celery, zucchini, carrot, mushrooms and garlic in olive oil. Cover, cook over low heat for 10 minutes. Add tomatoes, tomato paste and vegetable broth. Stir well. Add pepper; boil. Cover and cook over low heat for 1 hour, stirring occasionally. Add cooked pasta, chickpeas, kidney beans, green beans, basil and cabbage. Simmer 30 minutes. If desired, serve with Parmesan cheese.

Susan Cegelka
Waterbury, CT

Garden Minestrone Soup

Chunky Mushroom Chili

1 lb. lean ground beef
2 cups chopped onion
3 cloves garlic, minced
2 (16-oz.) cans tomatoes, chopped, undrained
2 (15-oz.) cans kidney beans, rinsed, drained
1 lb. fresh mushrooms, quartered
1 cup picante sauce
2 T. chili powder
2 tsp. ground cumin
1 ¼ tsp. salt
¾ tsp. dried oregano leaves
Grated cheddar cheese

Brown beef with onion and garlic. Drain excess fat. Add remaining ingredients except grated cheese; boil. Reduce heat, cover; simmer 30 minutes, stirring occasionally. Serve; topped with grated cheese.

Deanna Irwin
Munds Park, AZ

Stephanie's Garden Vegetable Soup

3 qts. water
1 lb. soup meat with beef bone
4 celery stalks with tops, diced
4 medium potatoes, peeled, diced
1 large tomato
¼ cup peeled, diced carrots
¼ cup shucked peas
¼ cup shucked lima beans
¼ cup diced string beans
¼ cup corn
1 small onion, peeled, minced

Boil water. Place meat in boiling water. Cook until half done; remove and cube into ¾-inch pieces (leave bone in until ready to serve and then discard bone). Reduce heat after meat is half done; add celery and potatoes. Simmer 30 minutes. Add whole tomato; remove after 3 minutes. Remove skin; dice flesh. Add to soup, removing and discarding seeds. Add rest of vegetables; simmer for one hour.

Stephanie A. Linnell
Colonia, NJ

Vegetable Chili

2 T. salad oil

2 medium green peppers, chopped

1 medium onion, chopped

1 medium zucchini, chopped

1 medium yellow straightneck squash, chopped

2 T. chili powder

1 T. sugar

¾ tsp. salt

¼ tsp. ground red pepper

2 (14 ½-oz.) cans stewed tomatoes

4-oz. can mild green chiles, chopped

2 (15-oz.) cans pinto beans

2 (15-oz.) cans black beans

2 cups corn

In 5-quart Dutch oven heat oil over medium heat. Cook pepper and onion until tender. Add zucchini, squash, chili powder, sugar, salt and ground red pepper. Cook 1 minute. Add stewed tomatoes with liquid, green chili, pinto beans with liquid, black beans with liquid and corn. Heat to boiling. Reduce heat to medium-low. Simmer uncovered for 20 minutes.

Mary Spanholtz
Eau Claire, MI

Vegetable Medley Soup

3 T. vegetable oil
28-oz. can stewed tomatoes
10-oz. can Rotel tomatoes
2 (28-oz.) cans water
10-oz. can water
1 large onion, chopped
5-6 Irish potatoes, chopped
1 tsp. black pepper
1 T. salt
1 T. sugar
½ lb. frozen okra, sliced
½ medium head cabbage, chopped
15 ¼-oz. can whole kernel corn

In large saucepan, combine oil, tomatoes, water, onion, potatoes, pepper, salt and sugar. Bring to a boil. Reduce heat to low; cook until vegetables are almost done. Add okra, cabbage and corn. Cook until vegetables are done.

L.N. Sowell
Huntsville, TX

Chicken and Rice Soup

4 pound fryer chicken, skinned, cut-up
2 quarts water
1 medium onion, chopped
2 stalks celery, sliced
1 tsp. salt
1 tsp. pepper
1 bay leaf
¾ cup uncooked long grain rice
1 carrot, diced

Combine first 7 ingredients in Dutch oven; boil. Cover; reduce heat. Simmer 45 minutes. Remove chicken from Dutch oven, reserving broth. Discard bay leaf. Set chicken aside. Add rice and carrot to broth; boil. Cover, reduce heat and simmer 20 minutes. Bone chicken; cut into bite size pieces. Add chicken to broth; heat thoroughly.

Anita Mills
Wichita Falls, TX

Vegetable and Cheese Chowder

6 T. margarine

¼ cup chopped onion

1 cup chopped green pepper

1 cup chopped celery

1 cup shredded carrot

1 cup shredded potato

10-oz. pkg. frozen peas

5 T. flour

3 cups water

1 T. chicken bouillon

3 cups grated cheddar cheese

2 cups milk

Parsley, chopped

½ tsp. salt

Freshly ground pepper

Melt margarine in pan. Sauté vegetables for 5 minutes, stirring constantly. Remove from heat; stir in flour. Add water and bouillon; boil stirring constantly. Simmer until vegetables are tender. Gradually stir in cheese until melted. Add milk gradually; heat, but do not boil. Sprinkle generously with parsley. Salt and pepper to taste.

Connie Snell
Grand Rapids, MI

Tomato Soup

¼ cup chopped onion

¼ cup chopped celery

2 T. margarine

2 cups chopped tomatoes, skin removed

1 ½ cups chicken broth

1 tsp. crushed thyme

½ tsp. sugar

1 bay leaf, split

Salt

Pepper

14-oz. can diced tomatoes with juice

1 cup milk

Cook onion, celery and margarine until tender. Add remaining ingredients except milk; boil. Reduce heat; simmer for 30 minutes. Cool slightly. Add milk. Remove bay leaf. Process in blender until smooth. Top with sour cream, shredded cheddar cheese or lemon slice.

Ruth Brendel
Palos Park, IL

breads

Garden Loaf

Garden Loaf

3 cups flour

1 ½ cups sugar

1 cup chopped walnuts

4 ½ tsp. baking powder

1 tsp. salt

4 eggs

1 cup shredded zucchini

1 cup shredded carrots

⅔ cup salad oil

2 tsp. grated lemon peel

Grease two loaf pans. Mix flour, sugar, walnuts, baking powder and salt in large bowl. In separate bowl, beat eggs slightly. Stir in zucchini, carrots, oil and lemon peel. Stir into flour mixture just until flour is moistened. Spread batter evenly in pans. Bake at 350 degrees for 1 hour. Serve warm.

Suzanne Johnston
Marinette, WI

Winter Squash Bread

2 pkg. dry yeast

1 cup warm milk

4-5 cups flour

2 cups whole-wheat flour

2 cups mashed, cooked, winter squash

¼ cup sugar

2 T. soft butter

2 tsp. salt

Dissolve yeast in milk in large mixing bowl. Add two cups flour. Add next 5 ingredients; beat until smooth. Add remaining flour. Turn out onto floured board; knead. Place in oiled bowl. Cover; let rise. Shape into loaves; place in 3 greased loaf pans. Let rise again. Bake at 375 degrees for 30-35 minutes.

Belle Stapleton
Dearing, KS

Mini-Chocolate Chip and Coconut Zucchini Loaves

3 eggs

2 cups sugar

½ cup vegetable oil

2 tsp. vanilla extract

2 cups unpeeled, shredded zucchini

3 cups flour

1 tsp. baking powder

1 tsp. baking soda

1 cup mini-chocolate chips

1 cup coconut

Combine eggs, sugar, vegetable oil and vanilla. Stir in zucchini. Combine flour, baking powder and baking soda. Add to egg mixture. Stir in chocolate chips and coconut. Divide between 16 mini-loaf pans and bake at 350 degrees for 20-30 minutes.

Michele Tabone
Brockway, PA

Rose Muffins

Rose Muffins

½ cup grated Monterey Jack cheese

¾ cup rose petals, washed

1 ¾ cups flour

2 ½ tsp. baking powder

1 T. sugar

¼ tsp. salt

1 egg

1 cup milk

3 T. margarine, melted

2 T. finely chopped pecans

Blend all ingredients. Fill muffin tins. Bake at 350 degrees for 30 minutes.

Susan Ann Olson
Garden Valley, ID

Bread Machine Zucchini Bread

⅓ cup plus 1 T. water

1 ½ cups grated zucchini

1 ½ cloves garlic, minced

3 T. grated cheddar cheese

¾ cup whole-wheat flour

2 ⅔ cups bread flour

¾ tsp. salt

1 ½ tsp. dry yeast

Add all ingredients to bread machine in order listed above. Follow your manufacturer's directions for baking bread.

Mrs. Sue Ellen Rabeaux
Youngsville, LA

Cherry Nut Zucchini Bread

3 eggs

2 cups sugar

½ tsp. almond extract

¼ cup vegetable oil

2 cups unpeeled, shredded zucchini

3 cups flour

1 tsp. baking powder

1 tsp. baking soda

½ cup quartered maraschino cherries

¾ cup chopped walnuts

Combine eggs, sugar, almond extract and vegetable oil. Stir in zucchini. In separate bowl, combine flour, baking powder and baking soda. Add to egg mixture. Stir in cherries and walnuts. Divide between 2 large loaf pans. Bake at 350 degrees for 50-55 minutes.

Michele Tabone
Brockway, PA

Zucchini Bread

3 eggs

1 cup oil

2 cups sugar

3 tsp. vanilla extract

2 cups grated zucchini

3 cups flour

¼ tsp. baking powder

1 tsp. baking soda

1 tsp. cinnamon

Combine all ingredients. Bake at 325 degrees for 1 hour.

Jennifer Tifft
Valley City, ND

Zucchini Apple Bread

4 cups flour
1 T. baking soda
1 1/2 T. ground cinnamon
1/4 tsp. baking powder
1/2 tsp. nutmeg
5 eggs
1 1/2 cups vegetable oil
2 cups sugar
1 cup firmly packed brown sugar
1 T. vanilla extract
2 cups shredded zucchini
1 cup shredded apple
1 1/2 cups chopped pecans

Combine first 5 ingredients; set aside. Combine eggs, oil, sugar, brown sugar and vanilla in large bowl. Beat at medium speed until well blended. Stir in zucchini, apple and pecans. Add dry ingredients; stir until just moistened. Use 3 greased and floured loaf pans. Bake at 350 degrees for 50-55 minutes.

Dona Branson
Greensboro, NC

breads

Strawberry Bread

3 eggs, beaten

1 cup vegetable oil

1 1/2 cups sugar

1 tsp. vanilla

2 cups mashed strawberries

3 cups flour

1 tsp. baking soda

1/4 tsp. baking powder

1 tsp. salt

1/2 cup chopped nuts

Combine eggs, oil, sugar and vanilla. Add strawberries. In separate bowl, sift together dry ingredients. Gradually add to strawberry mixture. Stir in nuts. Pour into two greased loaf pans. Bake at 325 degrees for 1 hour.

Suzanne McCloskey
Pottstown, PA

Strawberry Rhubarb Muffins

1 ¾ cups flour
½ cup sugar
2 ½ tsp. baking powder
¾ tsp. salt
1 egg, slightly beaten
¾ cup milk
⅓ cup vegetable oil
¾ cup minced, fresh rhubarb
½ cup sliced, strawberries
6 small strawberries, halved
Sugar

Combine flour, sugar, baking powder and salt in large bowl. Combine egg, milk and oil in separate bowl. Stir in flour mixture until just moistened. Fold rhubarb and sliced strawberries into batter. Fill muffin tins. Press a strawberry half gently into top of each muffin; sprinkle with sugar. Bake at 400 degrees for 20-25 minutes.

Janet Sprute
Lewiston, ID

Huckleberry Muffins

1 cup huckleberries
1 T. flour
½ cup butter
½ cup sugar
¾ cup milk
1 egg, slightly beaten
1 ¾ cups flour
2 ½ tsp. baking powder
½ tsp. salt

Toss huckleberries with 1 tablespoon flour. Cream together butter and sugar. Add milk and egg. Beat until smooth. Sift flour, baking powder and salt. Add to creamed mixture. Mix to combine; fold berries into batter. Fill greased muffin tins. Bake at 425 degrees for 20 minutes.

Martha Wickman
Casper, WY

Blueberry Muffins

½ cup butter

1 ¼ cups sugar

2 eggs

2 cups flour

2 tsp. baking powder

½ tsp. salt

½ cup milk

½ cup mashed blueberries

2 cups whole blueberries

2 tsp. sugar

Cream together butter and sugar until fluffy. Add eggs one at a time. Mix until blended. Sift dry ingredients; add alternately with milk. Add 1/2 cup mashed blueberries. Stir by hand; fold in remaining berries. Grease muffin tin. Pour batter into tin; sprinkle with 2 teaspoons sugar. Bake at 375 degrees for 25-30 minutes.

Edythe Boisvert
Amesbury, MA

side dishes

Italian Salad

Italian Salad

2 cups cooked green beans,
2 cups cooked yellow beans
1 medium cucumber, sliced
1 small zucchini, sliced
8 Roma tomatoes, sliced
6 small red skin potatoes, cooked, sliced
1 medium red onion, chopped
½ cup cider vinegar
½ cup olive oil
Optional: 2 cups broccoli, 1 T. fresh chives, 1 T. parsley, 1 T. oregano

Combine all ingredients. Marinate for 2 hours in refrigerator.

Nancy Kaufman
Saginaw, MI

Aloo Ghobi

5 medium white potatoes, peeled, chopped
1 large yellow onion, peeled, chopped
6 cloves garlic, peeled, chopped
2 cups water
1 head cauliflower, chopped
1 medium tomato, diced
1 cup chicken broth
1 tsp. ground cumin
½ tsp. cayenne pepper
1 ½ tsp. ground turmeric

Cook potatoes, onion and garlic in large covered pot with water for 20 minutes. Add remaining ingredients. Simmer mixture for 1 hour, stirring infrequently.

Christine Simmons
Seattle, WA

Sweet Potato Casserole

CASSEROLE:

3 cups boiled, mashed, sweet potatoes

1/3 cup milk

1/2 cup sugar

3 T. butter, softened

2 tsp. vanilla extract

2 eggs

Salt

TOPPING:

1 cup chopped pecans

1/2 cup brown sugar

1/3 cup flour

1 cup coconut

4 T. butter, melted

Mix together casserole ingredients; pour in 9 x 13-inch pan. Mix together topping ingredients; sprinkle over top. Bake at 350 degrees for 30 minutes.

Mrs. Roy Smith
Orange, TX

Carrots with Balsamic Vinegar

1 lb. carrots

2/3 cup water

1 1/2 T. butter, melted

Salt

Pepper

2 T. balsamic vinegar

Cut carrots into thin fingers. Add carrots and water to butter. Season with salt and pepper. Simmer, covered, for 5-6 minutes. Remove lid; turn up heat. Let liquid reduce to one tablespoon. Add balsamic vinegar. Stir well to coat carrots. Serve.

Kerrie Ann Skuran
Schaumburg, IL

Summer Pasta with Fresh Tomatoes and Herbs

Summer Pasta with Fresh Tomatoes and Herbs

¼ cup extra virgin olive oil

2 large ripe tomatoes, peeled, chopped

Kosher salt

Pepper

2 large cloves garlic, pressed

Dash of sugar

¼ tsp. crushed red pepper flakes

⅛ cup chopped fresh summer savory leaves

15 large fresh sweet basil leaves, chiffonade

⅛ cup chopped fresh thyme leaves

¼ cup dry white wine

Parmigiano-Reggiano cheese, shaved

½ lb. linguine, cooked

In sauté pan, heat olive oil and add tomatoes, salt and pepper. Sauté for 10 minutes. Add garlic, sugar and red pepper flakes. Sauté until combined. Add herbs; toss well. Add white wine; let reduce slightly. Add cheese, toss and serve over pasta.

Jill Freedman
Los Angeles, CA

Lemon Rice

1 cup chopped onion

¾ cup chopped green pepper

1 clove garlic, chopped

1 T. butter

1 cup uncooked long grain rice

1 ½ T. lemon juice

1 tsp. salt

¼ tsp. pepper

2 cups water

Sauté onions, green pepper and garlic in butter until tender-crisp. Add rice and remaining ingredients; boil. Stir well; cover, simmer 15 minutes or until rice is tender and liquid is absorbed.

Vivian Nikanow
Chicago, IL

Stuffed Italian Tomatoes

8 large tomatoes

1 cup chopped green onions

3 T. olive oil

1 1/2 cups chopped fresh spinach

1 cup ricotta cheese

2 egg yolks, beaten

1/2 cup chopped parsley

1/2 cup grated mozzarella cheese

1/2 cup grated Romano cheese

1/2 cup slivered almonds, toasted

Salt

Pepper

Wash tomatoes, remove tops; scrape out pulp. Salt cavity; turn upside down to drain for 30 minutes. Cook onions in oil 10 minutes over medium heat. Add spinach; stir until heated through. Remove from heat; set aside. In separate bowl, beat together ricotta cheese and egg yolks. Add parsley, mozzarella cheese, Romano cheese (reserve 1/4 cup) and slivered almonds. Season with salt and pepper. Stir in spinach mixture. Blend until all ingredients are well combined. Fill tomatoes with mixture; place stuffed tomatoes in shallow greased baking dish. Sprinkle tops with remaining Romano cheese. Bake for 20 minutes at 350 degrees or until tops are brown.

Marie L. Colasurdo
Portland, OR

Sliced Baked Potatoes

4 medium potatoes

1 tsp. salt

2-3 T. butter, melted

2-3 T. chopped fresh herbs (thyme, chives, sage, parsley)

4 T. grated cheddar cheese

1 1/2 T. Parmesan cheese

Cut potatoes into thin slices, but don't cut all the way through. Place potatoes in baking dish, slightly fanned. Sprinkle with salt; drizzle with butter. Sprinkle with herbs. Bake at 425 degrees for 50 minutes. Remove from oven; sprinkle with cheeses. Bake potatoes for another 10-15 minutes, until slightly browned.

Sheila Kottke
Torrance, CA

Shrimp Fettucine with Sun-Dried Tomatoes

½ cup sun-dried tomatoes
12 medium shrimp, peeled, deveined
3 T. olive oil
2 cloves garlic, minced
4 T. white wine
½ cup chicken stock
4 cups cooked fettucine
4 T. chopped, divided, fresh basil
Salt
White pepper
Grated Parmesan cheese

Soak tomatoes in hot water until softened. Sauté shrimp in olive oil until nearly cooked. Add garlic; cook until light brown. Add white wine to deglaze pan and stop garlic from browning further. Add chicken stock, sun-dried tomatoes, fettucine and half the basil. Cook briefly to reduce sauce. Season with salt and white pepper to taste. Serve garnished with remaining tablespoon of basil and a sprinkling of Parmesan cheese.

Carolyn L. Volturo
Sapulpa, OK

Fried Corn on the Cob

6 ears of corn, halved
2 cups flour
½ tsp. sugar
Salt
Pepper
1 egg
Water
Oil

Boil corn; let cool. Mix all remaining ingredients with enough water to make medium-thick batter. Roll corn in batter; deep fry until golden brown.

Note: Use this recipe for onion rings, shrimp, fried green tomatoes, etc.

Janice Windham
Seminary, MS

side dishes

Southern France Green Beans

1 lb. fresh green beans

1 yellow onion, chopped

4 cloves garlic, chopped

2 T. olive oil

½ cup dry white wine

4 large tomatoes, peeled, seeded, chopped

½ cup chopped black olives

1 T. fresh lemon juice

Black pepper, coarsely ground

Blanch green beans in boiling water until tender (3-4 minutes). Drain; rinse under cold water. Beans should be crispy. Set aside. Cook onion and garlic in oil for 5 minutes over low heat in deep skillet. Add wine and tomatoes. Cook for 20 minutes; stirring occasionally. Add reserved green beans and olives to the skillet. Heat thoroughly. Add lemon juice and pepper to taste. Serve immediately.

Rita Schaier
Allison Park, PA

Veggie Pasta Toss

1 green pepper, chopped

1 red tomato, chopped

1 cucumber, chopped

1 cup feta cheese

½ red onion, chopped

Italian dressing

2 cups cooked rotini pasta

1 cup chopped pepperoni

Toss all ingredients in large bowl. Chill at least 3 hours before serving.

Carol Comegys
Rochester, NY

Vegetable Antipasto

VEGETABLES:

1 cup peeled, angle-cut carrots

½ lb. fresh mushrooms

1 can small artichoke hearts, drained, halved

1 can large olives, drained, pitted

DRESSING:

⅔ cup white vinegar

⅔ cup olive oil

¼ cup finely chopped onion

2 cloves garlic, crushed

1 tsp. salt

1 tsp. sugar

1 tsp. dried basil leaves

1 tsp. dried oregano leaves

¼ tsp. coarse ground pepper

Parboil carrots until tender-crisp. Drain; cool. Combine dressing ingredients; boil. Simmer 10 minutes. Cool 15 minutes. Pour over vegetables layered in dish with tight seal. Chill overnight; turning occasionally to coat well. Toss gently; drain to serve.

Marian McCann
Salt Lake City, UT

Onion Pie

½ stick butter

1 cup finely crushed saltine crackers

¼ stick butter

3 cups thinly sliced onions

2 eggs, slightly beaten

¾ cup milk

1 tsp. salt

Dash of pepper

½ cup shredded sharp cheddar cheese

Put 1/2 stick butter in 9-inch pie plate. Placed in 300 degree oven for 5 minutes to melt butter. Pour cracker crumbs into pie plate; mix with fork. Form crust on bottom and sides; set aside. Melt 1/4 stick of butter in skillet; add onions. Cook over medium heat. Stir occasionally until onions are tender. Pour onions into pie shell. Beat eggs lightly with fork. Add milk, salt and pepper. Stir over medium heat until hot; do not boil. Pour over onions. Sprinkle with cheese. Bake at 350 degrees for 30 minutes.

Jacci Boardman
Hinckley, OH

Zucchini Crescent Bake

4 cups thinly sliced zucchini

1 cup chopped onion

½ cup butter

½ cup chopped parsley

½ tsp. salt

½ tsp. pepper

¼ tsp. garlic powder

¼ tsp. dried basil

½ tsp. dried oregano

2 eggs, beaten

8-oz. shredded mozzarella cheese

8-oz. can crescent rolls

2 tsp. Dijon mustard

Sauté zucchini and onion in butter for 10 minutes. Stir in parsley and seasonings. In separate bowl, beat eggs. Add cheese; combine with other ingredients. Separate crescent rolls; line 9 x 13-inch pan with dough. Press rolls up on the sides about 1 inch. Spread Dijon mustard on crust. Pour zucchini mixture into crust. Bake at 375 degrees for 18-20 minutes.

Jacqueline Craigo
Pine River, MN

Onion Pie

Tomatoes Stuffed with Antipasto Salad

Tomatoes

½ lb. Italian hard salami

½ lb. prosciutto

4 oz. Parmigiano-Reggiano cheese or provolone shavings

¼ cup chopped flat-leaf parsley leaves

Salt

Pepper

12 leaves fresh oregano, chopped

8 leaves fresh basil, chiffonade

Dash of sugar

2 handfuls chickpeas

2 roasted red or yellow peppers, chopped

¼ cup chopped kalamata or other pitted black olive

4 pepperoncini, whole

Extra virgin olive oil

Balsamic vinegar or red wine vinegar

Cut off tops of tomatoes, reserve. Squeeze tomatoes gently to remove seeds. With paring knife, cut away inner flesh; reserve. Slice meats into ¼-inch strips. Place meat in bowl with cheese. Add remaining ingredients except pepperoncini, olive oil and vinegar. Add reserved tomato flesh. Add olive oil and vinegar; toss and coat. Stuff tomatoes with mixture. Place pepperoncini and tomato cap on top. Serve on bed of lettuce with crusty Italian bread.

Jill Freedman
Los Angeles, CA

Garden Vegetable Pilaf

2 tsp. vegetable oil
2 cups long grain brown rice
4 cups broth or water
2 cups fresh vegetables (green onions, broccoli, celery, peppers, peas, etc.)
½ cup pine nuts
Herbs of choice
Salt
Pepper

Heat oil in heavy skillet over medium heat. Add rice. Stir for 5 minutes. Add broth. Cover tightly; cook for 45 minutes. Stir in remaining ingredients. Cover; cook for 5 more minutes.

Belle Stapleton
Dearing, KS

Marinated Carrots

2 lbs. carrots, sliced
1 small green pepper, thinly sliced
1 medium onion, thinly sliced
1 can tomato soup
½ cup oil
¾ cup sugar
¾ cup cider vinegar
1 tsp. prepared mustard
1 tsp. Worcestershire sauce
1 tsp. salt
½ tsp. pepper

Cook carrots until just tender. Drain; cool. In shallow dish alternate layers of carrots, peppers and onions. Combine all other ingredients; pour over vegetables. Refrigerate overnight.

Evelyn C. Burandt
Benton Harbor, MI

side dishes

Corn Soufflé

Corn Soufflé

1 T. butter, melted

2 T. flour

1 cup milk

2 cups corn

2 egg yolks, beaten

1 ½ tsp. salt

¼ tsp. freshly cracked black pepper

2 egg whites, beaten until stiff

Mix butter and flour. Add milk; stir and bring to a boil. Add corn and egg yolks. Season with salt and pepper. Cook for 10 minutes; fold in egg whites. Spoon into an unbuttered baking dish. Bake at 350 degrees for 40 minutes.

Kerrie Ann Skuran
Schaumburg, IL

Squash Supreme

4 squash, boiled

1 can cream of chicken soup

1 cup sour cream

1 carrot, grated

1 onion, chopped

Salt

Pepper

Butter

1 pkg. Pepperidge Farm Dressing

Mash squash, add soup, sour cream, carrot, onion, salt and pepper. Butter casserole dish, sprinkle thin layer of dressing on bottom. Add squash mix. Cover with additional dressing; dot with butter. Bake uncovered at 350 degrees for 30-40 minutes.

Pam Faulk
Concord, NC

Zucchini Country Style

1 T. salad oil

1 medium onion, diced

4 tomatoes, peeled, seeded, quartered

1 green pepper, chopped

1 small clove garlic

Salt

2 lbs. zucchini, peeled, cubed

Parmesan cheese, grated

Heat oil in large saucepan. Sauté onion until golden. Add tomatoes, green pepper and garlic; stir. Salt to taste. Cook over low heat about 15 minutes. Remove garlic; add cubed zucchini. Cover; simmer until zucchini is tender. Sprinkle with cheese before serving.

Betty Hofferber
Lexington, NE

Piccadilly Cafeteria's Carrot Soufflé

1 ¾ lbs. carrots, peeled

1 cup sugar

1 ½ tsp. baking powder

1 ½ tsp. vanilla

2 T. flour

3 eggs

1 stick margarine, room temperature

Powdered sugar

Steam or boil carrots until soft; drain well. Transfer to large mixing bowl. Add sugar, baking powder and vanilla. Beat with mixer until smooth. Add flour; mix well. Beat eggs for 5 minutes, add to carrot mixture. Beat well. Add margarine; blend well. Pour into two quart baking dish. Bake at 350 degrees for 1 hour or until top is light golden brown. Sprinkle with powdered sugar for garnish.

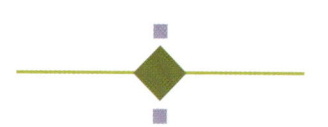

Dorris Medlin
Annandale, VA

main dishes

Rosemary's Chicken

Rosemary's Chicken

Chicken, skinned

6-8 red potatoes, chopped

1 T. rosemary

¼-⅓ cup olive oil

1 tsp. chopped garlic

⅓ cup chopped onion

1 pint cherry tomatoes

Salt

Pepper

Place chicken and potatoes in baking pan. In separate bowl mix rosemary, olive oil, garlic, onions and cherry tomatoes. Mix well. Pour over potatoes and chicken. Salt and pepper. Bake at 350 degrees for 1 hour 20 minutes.

J. Strausser
Bloomsburg, PA

Rice, Cheese and Tomato Casserole

Salt

1 tsp. sugar

Pepper

1 tsp. onion juice

2 cups strained tomatoes

Butter

2 cups rice, cooked

½ lb. grated cheese

Add salt, sugar, pepper and onion juice to tomatoes. Cover bottom of buttered baking dish with rice. Sprinkle liberally with cheese; pour tomato mixture over rice. Bake at 350 degrees for 30 minutes.

Mary Perkins-Clemons
Bloomington, IN

Pancit Noodles with Vegetables (Filipino Cuisine)

1 pkg. Pancit noodles

Water or stock

8 oz. shrimp

8 oz. beef, thinly sliced

3 T. vegetable oil

3 cloves garlic, minced

½ cup diced onions

1 lb. assorted vegetables, chopped (carrots, celery, cauliflower, cabbage, snow peas, onions, mushrooms, etc.)

¼ cup soy sauce

Drop noodles in 6 cups stock or boiling water. Separate noodles with fork; cook one minute. Drain; set aside. Cook shrimp and beef in oil. Add garlic, onions, vegetables and soy sauce. Stir in noodles. Remove from heat; serve.

Note: Pancit noodles may be found at a Filipino Oriental market.

Elizabeth Hines
Pittsburg, CA

Zucchini and Clam Casserole

Zucchini and Clam Casserole

2 cans minced clams
2 lbs. zucchini, peeled, sliced
Butter
16 saltine crackers
Freshly ground pepper
Light cream

Drain clams; reserve juice. Parboil and drain zucchini. Butter casserole dish. Crumble 8 saltines; spread on bottom of casserole dish. Mix clams and zucchini. Season well with pepper; pour into casserole dish. Add 8 more crumbled saltines. Dot with butter. Add cream to clam juice to make 1 cup of liquid. Pour over zucchini mixture. Bake at 350 degrees for 35-40 minutes.

Catherine Whitcomb
Newport, VT

Upside Down Vegetable Dish

2 cups flour
2 tsp. baking powder
1/2 tsp. salt
1/4 cup shortening
1 egg, beaten
1 cup milk
4 cups mixed, cooked vegetables, 1/2 cup liquid reserved
2 T. butter
Optional: 1 cup hot tomato sauce

Grease shallow 2 quart baking dish. Combine flour, baking powder and salt. Cut in shortening. Combine egg and milk. Add to dry ingredients, stirring constantly. Arrange vegetables in baking dish. Pour vegetable liquid over vegetables. Dot with butter. Cover with flour mixture. Bake at 425 degrees for 20-25 minutes. Turn onto hot platter with vegetables on top. Serve hot with tomato sauce.

Vivian Nikanow
Chicago, IL

Shipwreck

1 qt. raw potatoes, diced
3 T. butter
1 large onion, diced
1 can kidney beans
¼ cup uncooked rice
1 ½ cups diced tomatoes
2 tsp. salt
¼ tsp. pepper
½ cup water
1 lb. hamburger

Place potatoes in buttered casserole dish. Mix together next 7 ingredients. Crumble hamburger on top. Bake at 350 degrees for 1 1/2 hours.

Evelyn Overkamp
Rhineland, MO

Garden Delight

½ head cabbage, shredded
8 potatoes, chopped
8 carrots, sliced
1 onion, chopped
½ red bell pepper, chopped
1 lb. kielbasa, chopped
2 T. chopped parsley

1 T. minced garlic
1 T. olive oil
2-3 qts. water
4 chicken bouillon cubes
Salt
Pepper

Combine ingredients in large saucepan. Boil for 30 minutes. Serve.

Todd P. Johnson
Laurel, MD

Sausage and Peppers

4 green peppers, chopped

2 large onions, chopped

3 T. olive oil

1 lb. mild or hot Italian sausage

Salt

Pepper

1 cup white wine

Rolls

Sauté peppers and onions in olive oil until slightly tender. Remove from skillet; set aside. Add sausage; brown. Place sausage in baking dish; sprinkle with salt and pepper. Pour wine on top; cover. Bake at 350 degrees for 45-60 minutes. Uncover; add sautéed vegetables. Bake, uncovered 30 minutes more. Serve in rolls.

Vivian Nikanow
Chicago, IL

Vegetables and Rice

½ lb. sliced beef

1 T. oil

1 T. cornstarch

⅛ tsp. pepper

½ tsp. salt

1 cup beef broth

1 cup shredded cabbage

1 cup shredded carrots

1 small onion, chopped

2 cups rice, cooked

Cook beef in oil. Add cornstarch, pepper, salt and beef broth. Mix well. Add cabbage, carrots and onion. Cook until thickened. Serve over rice.

Lucille Howard
Hendersonville, NC

Old South Jambalaya

Oil

2 cups chopped onion

½ cup chopped bell pepper

½ cup chopped parsley

2 cups tomato sauce

2 cups beer

3 tsp. salt

Pepper

Desired spices (cayenne pepper, minced garlic, chives, cilantro, celery flakes, etc.)

2 cups water

2 cups rice, uncooked

4 cups diced Cajun sausage

Heat oil in large saucepan. Add onion, bell pepper and parsley. Sauté until tender. Add tomato sauce, beer, salt, pepper and spices. Heat until warm. Add water, rice and sausage. Cook over medium heat for 30 minutes.

Sharon Elder
Perry, KS

Pasta Fazool

1 lb. pasta

4 medium onions, chopped

2 large carrots, chopped

3 large ribs celery, chopped

6-10 cloves garlic, diced

8 slices pancetta

2 T. olive oil

1 qt. tomatoes, chopped

½ tsp. crushed, dried rosemary

1 tsp. oregano

½ tsp. basil

1 T. parsley

2 (15-oz.) cans northern beans or navy beans

Romano Cheese

Cook pasta al dente. Drain water, leaving just enough to cover pasta by ½ inch. Sauté onions, carrots, celery, garlic and pancetta in olive oil. Add sautéed ingredients to pasta along with tomatoes, rosemary, oregano, basil, parsley and beans. Simmer 20 minutes. Add Romano cheese; simmer 10 more minutes.

Tina Walker
Pittsburgh, PA

Old South Jambalaya

Country Goulash

1 lb. hamburger

1 lb. sausage, chopped

1 large onion, chopped

Garlic powder

4-5 large potatoes, thinly sliced

1 small head cabbage, sliced

Seasoned salt

Smoke flavor

1 cup water

Brown meats and onion. Sprinkle with garlic powder. Drain; rinse well. Place browned meat in large skillet. Layer potatoes over meat. Layer cabbage over potatoes. Sprinkle seasoned salt and smoke flavor. Slowly pour water over top of casserole. Simmer for approximately 1 hour; until cabbage and potatoes are cooked.

Dana Duvall
Youngsville, NC

Chicken Piccata

6 boneless chicken breast halves

1 T. flour

1 tsp. salt

1 T. fresh tarragon

3 T. butter

½ cup chicken broth

3 lemon slices, halved

Rice or pasta

1 T. finely minced fresh parsley

Cut each chicken breast half into 10 or 12 strips. Combine flour, salt and tarragon in small custard cup. Melt butter in large skillet over high heat. Add chicken strips. Sprinkle with flour mixture. Cook 5 minutes on high heat, stirring constantly. Add chicken broth and lemon slices; stir to loosen any brown particles. Cover; cook 3-5 minutes. Serve over rice, pasta or buttered toast. Sprinkle with parsley.

Kay Tibbs
Pickerington, OH

Pescado Fabiola

1 medium onion, finely diced
1 medium bell pepper, finely diced
1 large ripe tomato, seeded, diced
2 T. butter
2 T. flour
1-1 ½ cups milk
4-6 (3-inch by 4-inch) portions mild, firm fish, 1-inch thick (grouper works well)
Salt
Pepper

In large, heavy skillet, sauté vegetables in butter over medium heat. Mash vegetables into pulp. When there is more pulp than solid pieces, stir in flour. When flour is absorbed, slowly add milk; stir constantly until sauce thickens. Add fish; cook no more than 10 minutes, turning fish once. Salt and pepper to taste.

Cora Raiford
Jacksonville, FL

Micro Beef Tostada Pie

1 ½ lbs. ground beef
1 onion, chopped
1 green pepper, chopped
1 ½ tsp. chili powder
¾ tsp. salt
¼ tsp. garlic salt
1 tsp. cumin
8-oz. can tomato sauce
16-oz. can tomatoes, drained
2 cups crushed Doritos
1 cup shredded cheddar cheese

In microwave or on stove top, brown beef, onion and green pepper. Drain. Stir in seasonings, tomato sauce and tomatoes. Sprinkle 1 cup Doritos in bottom of 8-inch square pan sprayed with nonstick spray. Layer half the meat mixture, half the cheese, remaining Doritos, then remaining meat mixture. Cover and microwave 8 minutes. Top with extra cheese and whole Doritos.

Mary Young
Crestwood, KY

Mexican Zucchini Bake

¾-1 lb. garlic sausage or ground beef
1 T. margarine
2 zucchini or yellow crookneck squash
¼-½ lb. mushrooms
2 T. chopped onion
1 tsp. chili powder
1 tsp. salt
½ tsp. garlic powder
2 cups rice, cooked
1 can chopped green chile peppers
½ cup sour cream
1 cup shredded Jack or sharp cheddar cheese

Brown meat in skillet. Add margarine, zucchini, mushrooms and onion. Cook until tender. Drain. Stir in chili powder, salt and garlic powder. Add rice, chiles, sour cream and half the cheese. Transfer to 2 quart baking dish. Bake at 350 degrees for 20 minutes. Sprinkle with remaining cheese.

Anne Hagsten
Hibbing, MN

Herbed Chicken Breast

1 container whipped cream cheese
2 T. butter
1 T. chopped fresh parsley
2 T. chopped fresh chives
4 boneless chicken breasts, pounded thin
4 slices bacon

Mix together cream cheese, butter and herbs. Divide evenly into 4 parts. Place one part on each chicken breast and roll up. Wrap each chicken roll with one slice of bacon. Lay in glass baking dish. Bake uncovered at 350 degrees for 45 minutes.

Susan Crumbacher
Xenia, OH

Chicken Tarragon

½ cup flour
1 T. salt
½ tsp. pepper
⅛ tsp. paprika
2 frying chickens, chopped
½ cup butter, softened
1 cup finely chopped onion
1 tsp. finely crushed tarragon
1-2 cups mushrooms
1 cup dry white wine

Combine flour, salt, pepper and paprika. Dredge chicken in flour mixture. Melt butter in large skillet; add onion. Sauté until tender, but not brown. Remove from pan; set aside. Brown chicken. Remove from skillet; set in baking pan. Combine onion, tarragon and mushrooms. Spread evenly over chicken and pour white wine over top. Bake at 350 degrees for 45 minutes or until chicken is tender.

Daniel McDonald
Boise, ID

Chicken Breast in Sour Cream

6 chicken breast halves
1 stick margarine
½ cup chopped onion
1 cup chopped celery
1 green pepper, chopped
1 small can sliced mushrooms, drained, juice reserved
½ pint sour cream
Salt
Coarsely ground pepper

Remove skin from chicken; brown lightly in margarine. Place in large casserole dish. Sauté onion, celery, green pepper and mushrooms. Let cook; add sour cream and juice from mushrooms. Salt and pepper to taste. Ladle sauce over chicken breast. Bake, covered, at 350 degrees for 45 minutes. Serve with brown rice.

Voncile Tuttle
Bethpage, TN

Grilled Vegetables and Chicken Sandwich

Grilled Vegetables and Chicken Sandwich

Marinade:
½ cup soy sauce
2 tsp. sesame oil
2 T. olive oil
1 clove garlic
Salt
Pepper
2-3 green onions, chopped

Sandwich:
Boneless chicken breasts
1-2 red peppers, grilled, sliced
6-8 slices eggplant, grilled
6-8 slices onion, grilled

Combine marinade ingredients. Marinate vegetables and chicken for 2 hours. Grill vegetables and chicken. Make sandwich by layering chicken and vegetables on rolls or bread. Add slices of your favorite cheese.

Paul Caruolo
Cary, NC

Hamburger Pie

Pie:
1 lb. ground beef
1 medium onion, chopped
1 small green pepper, chopped
Salt
Pepper
1 can stewed tomatoes
1 small can tomato paste
1 can wax beans, drained

Topping:
5 medium potatoes
½ cup warm milk
1 egg, beaten
Salt
Pepper

Brown meat, onion and pepper. Add seasonings, stewed tomatoes, tomato paste and beans. Heat through. Pour into casserole dish. Cook potatoes; mash, add milk, egg, salt and pepper. Spoon into mounds on meat in casserole dish. Bake at 350 degrees for 20 minutes—until potato peaks turn brown.

Evelyn C. Burandt
Benton Harbor, MI

Camille's Eggplant Casserole

2 large eggplants, peeled, diced
1 large onion, chopped
1 bell pepper, chopped
3 T. light oil
½ lb. hot country-style sausage
1 ½ cups cooked rice
10-oz. can cheddar cheese soup
Seasoned salt

Cook eggplants in salt water until tender. Drain; set aside. Sauté onion and bell pepper in oil. Lightly mix all ingredients; spoon into 2 quart casserole dish. Sprinkle with seasoned salt. Bake at 350 degrees for 1 hour.

Camille Barmore
Pearland, TX

Green/Yellow Garden Wheel

1 lb. medium zucchini
1 lb. medium yellow squash
1 T. olive oil
½ stick butter, softened
1 tsp. chopped fresh chives
1 tsp. chopped fresh tarragon
1 tsp. chopped fresh thyme
Salt
Pepper
3 T. fresh bread crumbs
3 T. freshly grated Parmesan cheese
2 T. freshly grated Romano cheese

Cut each squash and zucchini lengthwise into four slices. Spread and alternate green and yellow slices in a circle on oiled pizza pan. In bowl, mix butter, herbs, salt and pepper. In separate bowl toss bread crumbs with Parmesan and Romano cheeses. Spread herb butter evenly over layers of vegetables. Sprinkle bread crumb and cheese mixture over layers. Broil (about 5 inches from the heat) 3 minutes or until golden brown.

Angeline Ingram
Annandale, VA

Cornish Pasties

1 lb. hamburger, browned, drained

5 cups cubed, potatoes, boiled (²/₃ done)

1 cup shredded carrots

1 cup diced onions

1 tsp. minced garlic

Salt

Pepper

4 pie crusts, unbaked

Mix meat, potatoes, carrots, onions, garlic and seasonings. Place one-fourth of mix near center on one side of each pie crust. Moisten bottom edge, pull top over and crimp edge with fork. Bake at 375 degrees for 50 minutes, or until golden brown. Serve with ketchup.

Thomas Boyer
Coldspring, TX

Stuffed Pumpkin

5 ½-6 lb. pumpkin

1 tsp. salt, divided

1 ½ lbs. hamburger

¾ cup chopped onion

1 small green pepper

Optional: hot pepper

1 ½ cups cooked rice

1 pint canned Roma tomatoes

2 eggs, beaten

1 clove garlic

1 tsp. oregano

½ tsp. black pepper

Salt

½ tsp. cider vinegar

Clean and remove seeds from pumpkin. Place in Dutch oven with ½ teaspoon salt and enough water to cover pumpkin. Cook 30 minutes. In skillet, brown beef, onion, green pepper and hot pepper. Add rice, tomatoes, eggs, garlic, oregano, black pepper, salt and vinegar. Place cooked pumpkin in shallow baking dish and firmly pack with meat mixture. Replace top. Leave pan uncovered. Bake at 350 degrees for 1 hour. Let stand 10-15 minutes before carving into wedges. Serve with mashed potatoes and tomato sauce.

Tammy Bowers
Gordonsville, VA

Mexican Vegetable Lasagna

MEXICAN SAUCE:

1 cup chopped onion

1 clove garlic, minced

2 T. margarine, melted

2 cups peeled, chopped tomatoes

¼ cup chopped green chile peppers

¼ cup chopped green pepper

8-oz. can tomato sauce

1 tsp. sugar

1 tsp. ground cumin

½ tsp. salt

½ tsp. oregano

½ tsp. basil

LASAGNA:

2 T. lemon juice

1 T. olive oil

1 medium eggplant, unpeeled, halved lengthwise, sliced

⅓ cup fine, dried Italian bread crumbs

¼ cup grated Parmesan cheese

½ cup part-skim ricotta cheese

¼ cup shredded part-skim mozzarella cheese

Preheat broiler. In small bowl, combine lemon juice and olive oil. Brush eggplant slices with the mixture; arrange in single layer on nonstick baking sheet. Broil 5-6 inches from heat for 2 1/2 minutes on each side or until golden brown.

Reduce baking temperature to 350 degrees. In small bowl, combine bread crumbs and Parmesan cheese. In separate bowl combine Mexican sauce ingredients. Spoon one-third Mexican sauce into deep flame-proof 1 1/2 quart casserole. Sprinkle with half of bread crumb mixture; cover with layer of eggplant. Spread half ricotta cheese over eggplant; continue to layer in same order, ending with sauce. Sprinkle mozzarella cheese on top. Bake for 45 minutes.

Nancy Roughley
Shelton, WA

Zucchini Casserole

6 cups cubed zucchini
¼ cup chopped onion
1 cup cream of chicken soup
1 cup sour cream
1 cup shredded carrots
1 pkg. Stove Top chicken stuffing
½ cup oleo, melted
1 cup shredded cheddar cheese

Cook zucchini and onion in boiling water for 5 minutes; drain. Combine soup and sour cream. Mix well. Stir in carrots, zucchini and onions. Combine stuffing and oleo. Spread half stuffing mixture in 9 x 13-inch pan. Spoon in vegetable mixture; sprinkle cheese over vegetables. Spread remaining stuffing on top. Bake at 350 degrees for 1 hour.

Dean & Debra Reid
Engadine, MI

Pork Chops with Rhubarb Dressing

PORK:
½ tsp. dried rosemary
¾ tsp. salt
⅛ tsp. pepper
6 pork chops
2 T. salad oil

DRESSING:
½-¾ cup brown sugar
4 slices bread, cubed
½ tsp. cinnamon
¼ tsp. allspice
3 T. flour
4 cups chopped rhubarb

Mix rosemary, salt and pepper. Rub on pork. Brown chops in oil; save drippings. Combine rest of ingredients. Spread half the mixture in greased 9 x 13-inch pan. Arrange chops on top. Spoon 3 tablespoons drippings on top. Top with remaining dressing. Bake, covered at 350 degrees for 45 minutes. Uncover; bake 15 more minutes.

Betty Nelson
Des Moines, IA

Lemon and Thyme Flounder

Flounder fillets
Lemon juice
Lemon pepper
Lemon thyme
Almond chips

Place fillets in cake pan. Sprinkle lemon juice and lemon pepper over fish. Place lemon thyme strips on fish (about 3 strips per fillet). Sprinkle with almond chips. Bake at 425 degrees for 15 minutes.

Melanie J. Budbill
Marshall, NC

Chicken Pot Pie

CRUST:
4 cups flour
1 T. sugar
1 ½ tsp. salt
1 ½ cups butter flavored shortening
1 egg
1 T. vinegar
½ cup cold water

PIE FILLING:
1 ½ cups butter
½-1 cup flour
1 ½ cups milk
½ lb. carrots
1 can peas, drained
1 can corn, drained
1 can green beans, drained
2 lbs. chicken, cooked, chopped
Salt
Pepper

To prepare crust, mix flour, sugar and salt. Add shortening using pastry blender. When dough looks like cornmeal, add egg, vinegar and water. Set aside.

To prepare filling, heat butter in saucepan. Add flour; whisk. Add milk. When mixture starts to thicken, add vegetables and chicken. Salt and pepper to taste. Cook until hot.

Roll dough to fit baking pan. Then roll dough for top crust. Pour chicken and vegetable filling into crust. Add top crust. Brush milk over top of crust with pastry brush. Bake at 350 degrees for 1 hour, until golden brown. Let cool 20 minutes; serve.

Sue Freed
Wapakoneta, OH

Lemon and Thyme Flounder

Chicken À La Tom

4 T. butter
2 cups thinly sliced celery
2/3 cup sliced green onion
1 cup mushrooms
4 cups chicken stock
(or 4 cups water and 4 bouillon cubes)
1 cup peas
2 cups thinly sliced carrots
2 cups diced cooked chicken
Salt
Pepper
1/4 tsp. celery powder
1/4 tsp. onion powder
1/4 tsp. garlic powder

Melt butter in large skillet over high heat. Add celery, onions and mushrooms; stir fry for 3 minutes. Add remaining ingredients; boil. Simmer until vegetables are tender. Thicken with cornstarch mixed with cold water if necessary. Serve with baking powder biscuits.

Thomas L. Boyer
Coldspring, TX

Whole Stuffed Pumpkin with Sausage

1 medium pumpkin
1 pkg. sausage
1 1/2 cups diced onion
1 1/2 cups diced celery
1 cup quartered cherry tomatoes
2 cups diced zucchini
1 cup corn kernels
1 1/2 cups kidney beans, cooked
1 1/2 tsp. chili powder
1/4 tsp. thyme
1/2 tsp. cumin
1 cup grated Monterey Jack cheese
Salt
Pepper

Clean and seed pumpkin as if to use for jack-o-lantern. Brown sausage. Sauté onion and celery. In large bowl, mix all ingredients except pumpkin. Spoon mixture into pumpkin and pack lightly. Cover with pumpkin lid and rub with vegetable oil. Bake at 350 degrees for 30-40 minutes.

Pati Fagan
Lancaster, CA

Spinach Cheese Pie

PIE SHELL:

1 1/2 cups hot, cooked rice

1 T. snipped chives

1 egg white

PIE FILLING:

6 eggs

1/2 cup milk

1/4 tsp. salt

1/4 tsp. pepper

Fresh spinach, chopped

Small onion, chopped

1/2 cup grated cheddar cheese

To make crust, mix rice, chives and egg white with fork. Spray 10-inch pie pan with nonstick spray. Turn crust ingredients into pie pan; spread evenly with rubber scraper. Bake at 350 degrees for 5 minutes.

To make filling, combine eggs, milk, salt and pepper; beat until foamy. Place spinach, onion and cheese in pie shell. Pour egg mixture into pie crust. Bake at 375 degrees for 30 minutes.

Mary Premo
Adams, WI

Tomato Pie

Dough:

2 cups flour

1 stick butter

4 tsp. baking powder

¾ cup milk

Filling:

2 lbs. tomatoes, peeled, thinly sliced

Basil

Chives

Scallions

Dill

1 ½ cups grated sharp cheddar cheese

⅓ cup mayonnaise

2 T. lemon juice

Blend all dough ingredients together in food processor until crumbly. Roll out half the dough on floured surface. Fit into 9-inch pie plate. Lay tomatoes over crust; sprinkle basil, chives, scallions and dill to taste. Sprinkle 1 cup cheese. Thin mayonnaise with lemon juice; drizzle over cheese. Top with remaining cheese. Roll out remaining crust. Fit over filling; pinch edges to seal. Cut slits in top; Bake at 400 degrees for 25 minutes.

P.L. Postallian
Cincinnati, OH

Stuffed Bell Peppers

3 large bell peppers

1 lb. lean ground beef

1 cup finely chopped potato

1 cup finely chopped onion

1 cup finely chopped cabbage

Salt

Pepper

1 pint tomatoes

1 pint tomato juice

Cut peppers in half lengthwise. Remove seeds. Mix together beef, potato, onion, cabbage, salt and pepper. Stuff each half pepper with beef mixture. Place in baking dish. Top each stuffed pepper with tomato, pour juice over top. Bake at 350 degrees for 1 hour.

Belle Stapleton
Dearing, KS

Lemon-Dill Turkey Pitas

1 pkg. lean ground turkey
1 medium onion, chopped
¼ tsp. dillweed
¼ tsp. black pepper
¼ tsp. grated lemon peel
2 T. lemon juice
2 T. water
1 ½ cups nonfat plain yogurt
¾ cup shredded carrot
1 tsp. dried dillweed
6 (6-inch) pocket breads, halved
2 cups chopped lettuce (or alfalfa sprouts)

Spray large skillet with nonstick cooking spray. Heat skillet over medium-high heat for 30 seconds. Crumble turkey into skillet. Add onion, dillweed, pepper and lemon peel. Cook and stir 3-5 minutes or until turkey is lightly browned and onion is tender. Add lemon juice and water. Cook 3-5 minutes or until liquid is absorbed. In a small bowl, combine yogurt, carrot and dried dillweed. Stir into turkey mixture. Fill each pocket bread half; add lettuce.

Sheila Kottke
Torrance, CA

Pueblo Wrap

Pueblo Wrap

1 red Roma tomato tortilla or spinach flour tortilla

6 oz. smoked turkey breast, sliced

2 slices bacon, fried (preferably thick-sliced)

½ avocado, sliced

Lettuce

Tomatoes, sliced

Red onions, sliced

Black bean salsa

Cilantro crème fraîche

Cilantro Crème Fraîche:

6 oz. sour cream

3 oz. heavy cream

½ bunch fresh cilantro, chopped

Black Bean Salsa:

8 oz. black beans

1 medium onion, diced

1 red bell pepper, diced

1 green bell pepper, diced

6 oz. corn, roasted

1 poblano chile, diced

3 oz. red wine vinegar

1 oz. lemon juice

1 oz. fresh garlic, minced

1 bunch cilantro, chopped

1 oz. chili powder

2 oz. cumin

Salt

Pepper

To make Pueblo Wrap, place lettuce evenly over tortilla. Add turkey breast, tomatoes and onion. Add avocado and bacon. Distribute all ingredients evenly. Slowly roll tortilla into tight wrap. Cut on bias; garnish with crème fraîche, black bean salsa and fresh cilantro leaves.

To make cilantro crème fraîche, combine sour cream, heavy cream and cilantro. Puree all ingredients in food processor until smooth. Chill.

To make black bean salsa, combine all ingredients; let stand in refrigerator overnight.

Carolyn L. Volturo
Sapulpa, OK

Stuffed Cabbage Rolls

12 large cabbage leaves
1 ¼ lbs. ground beef
2 tsp. salt
½ tsp. pepper
1 cup cooked rice
1 small onion, chopped
1 egg
½ tsp. poultry seasoning or thyme
2 T. vegetable oil
2 (8-oz.) cans tomato sauce
1 T. brown sugar
¼ cup water
1 T. lemon juice or vinegar

Cover cabbage leaves with boiling water; let stand for 5 minutes or until limp. Drain. Combine next 7 ingredients. Place equal portions of meat mixture in center of each leaf. Fold side of each leaf over meat. Roll up; fasten with toothpicks or string. Brown in large skillet in hot oil. Add tomato sauce to skillet. Combine brown sugar, water and lemon juice; stir into tomato sauce. Simmer, uncovered for 1 hour, basting occasionally.

Dorris Medlin
Annandale, VA

Zucchini and Tomato Casserole

1 large zucchini, sliced
3 large tomatoes, peeled, sliced
1 large sweet onion, sliced
1 ½ cups cracker crumbs
Salt
Pepper
1 cup grated sharp cheddar cheese
1 stick margarine
1 T. brown sugar

Alternate layers of zucchini, tomato and onion in buttered casserole dish. Sprinkle layers with crackers, salt, pepper and cheese. Dot with bits of margarine. Sprinkle tomato layer with brown sugar. Sprinkle top with cheese. Bake at 350 degrees for 1 hour.

Marianne Holdeman
Bloomington, IN

Creole Chicken Pie

PASTRY:
1 cup flour
½ tsp. salt
⅓ cup shortening
2 T. ice cold water

FILLING:
1 lb. ground chicken
2 T. olive oil
3 cloves garlic, chopped
½ cup flour
1 tsp. salt
¼ tsp. pepper
1 qt. canned tomatoes
½ cup chopped green pepper
¾ cup sliced onion
1 ½ cups diced celery

To make pastry, mix flour and salt; cut in shortening. Add ice water. Mix well; form into ball. Roll out to fit casserole. Cut slits for air.

To make filling, brown chicken in oil with half of garlic. Stir in flour, salt, pepper and tomatoes. Add peppers, onion, celery and remaining garlic; boil. Pour into 1 1/2 quart casserole dish. Cover with pastry topping. Fold pastry under; flute edges just inside dish. Bake at 425 degrees 30-35 minutes.

B. Harding
San Jose, CA

Mexican Eggplant

1 large eggplant, peeled, sliced

¼ cup vegetable oil

15-oz. can tomato sauce

4-oz. can chopped, mild green chile peppers

1 small can ripe olives, sliced

¼-½ cup chopped green onion

½ tsp. ground cumin

½ tsp. garlic salt

1-1 ½ cups grated cheddar cheese

Optional: 1 cup sour cream

Brush sides of eggplant slices with oil. Place in single layer on greased baking sheet. Bake at 450 degrees for 20 minutes. Combine tomato sauce, chiles, olives, green onion, cumin and garlic salt in saucepan. Simmer, uncovered for 10 minutes. In flat greased casserole dish, layer eggplant, sauce and cheese. Bake uncovered at 350 degrees for 20-25 minutes. Serve with sour cream, if desired.

Jean Fields
Apple Valley, CA

Eggplant Italiano

1 medium eggplant, peeled, sliced

4 medium very ripe tomatoes, cored, sliced

3 tsp. finely minced garlic

1 tsp. oregano

1 tsp. basil

1 tsp. crushed rosemary

Salt

2 T. olive oil

1 cup plain or Italian seasoned bread crumbs

8-oz. pkg. low-fat mozzarella cheese

Alternate layers of eggplant and tomato compactly in lightly oiled baking dish. Sprinkle garlic, herbs and salt over each layer. Drizzle olive oil over top layer. Sprinkle with bread crumbs; top with mozzarella cheese. Bake at 450 degrees for 30 minutes, basting several times.

Cora Raiford
Jacksonville, FL

main dishes

Zucchini Pizza

DOUGH:

4 cups grated zucchini

2 eggs, beaten

1 cup grated cheddar cheese

TOPPING:

1 lb. hamburger

1 small onion, diced

1 tsp. oregano

Salt

Pepper

8-oz. can tomato sauce or paste

½ cup chopped mushrooms

1 cup grated cheese

Combine dough ingredients; spread in buttered pan or cookie sheet. Bake at 400 degrees for 10 minutes.

Brown meat and onion; drain. Add oregano, salt, pepper, tomato sauce and mushrooms. Spread on dough and top with cheese. Bake at 350 degrees for 20 minutes or until done.

Jeanne Walsh
Davenport, IA

Black Bean Burgers with Banana Ketchup

BLACK BEAN BURGERS:

2 (15-oz.) cans black beans, drained

½ tsp. garlic salt

1 T. olive oil, divided

½ cup chopped purple onion

1 sweet banana pepper, seeded, minced

1 clove garlic, minced

½ cup self-rising flour, divided

⅛ tsp. garlic pepper

½ tsp. cumin powder

Optional: ½ tsp. cayenne pepper

1 T. chopped oregano

1 T. chopped basil

1 T. chopped thyme

BANANA KETCHUP:

½ cup chopped yellow onion

½ T. vegetable oil

3 medium ripe bananas, mashed

⅓ cup apricot jam

¾ cup orange juice

1 T. firmly packed brown sugar

½ T. white vinegar

1 T. lime juice

Salt

Pepper

Place 1 can beans and ½ teaspoon garlic salt in food processor. Puree until smooth. Transfer mixture to medium bowl; set aside. Heat half of olive oil in nonstick sauté pan over medium heat. Add onion, banana pepper and garlic. Cook until onion is transparent. Add ¼ cup flour; cook 5 minutes, stirring constantly so it doesn't scorch. Add to bean puree in bowl. Add remaining beans, stir to combine; add garlic pepper. Form mixture into 6 patties. Place on wax paper lined paper plate. Cover with wax paper; refrigerate until firm (about 1 hour).

Preheat oven to 350 degrees. Heat remaining oil in nonstick sauté pan over medium heat. Combine remaining flour, cumin, cayenne and herbs in shallow dish. Coat patties with flour mixture; sauté until lightly crisp on each side. Transfer patties to baking sheet; place in oven until hot, about 5 minutes. Serve with banana ketchup.

To prepare banana ketchup, sauté onion in oil over medium heat until transparent, about 5 minutes. Add bananas; continue cooking for another 5 minutes. Add jam, orange juice and sugar; boil. Continue cooking until thickened, about 30 minutes; cool. Add vinegar, lime juice, salt and pepper.

Rosemary Johnson
Birmingham, AL

La Ratatouille Nicoise

2 lbs. Italian eggplants; quartered and cut in 1-inch pieces

Olive oil

2 lbs. Italian zucchinis, cut in ½-inch rounds

2 lbs. green peppers, cut in fine rounds

2 lbs. onions, minced

10 cloves garlic, minced

20 basil leaves, minced

5 pinches thyme

3 lbs. ripe tomatoes, crushed

Salt

Pepper

Sauté eggplant in 3 tablespoons olive oil until tender; set aside. Sauté zucchini, green peppers and onions in same manner. In deep casserole, sauté three-fourths of garlic and basil. Add thyme and tomatoes. Cook until bubbly. Pour sautéed vegetables into casserole; mix with tomatoes (without crushing vegetables). Simmer until all vegetables are tender. 15 minutes before serving, add remaining garlic and basil. Salt and pepper to taste. Mix and serve.

Mrs. Andree G. Joy
Carver, MA

Ann's Party Spinach

4 (10-oz.) pkg. frozen spinach, chopped

½ lb. mushrooms, sliced

2 T. butter

½ cup mayonnaise

½ cup sour cream

½ cup grated Parmesan cheese

8 ½-oz. can artichoke hearts, drained, quartered

Salt

Pepper

3 tomatoes, sliced

½ cup dried bread crumbs

¼ cup butter

Cook spinach to package directions; drain. Sauté mushrooms in 2 tablespoons butter. Combine mayonnaise, sour cream and cheese. Stir in artichokes, spinach and mushrooms. Salt and pepper to taste. Spread into 9 x 13-inch greased baking dish. Place tomatoes on spinach mixture. Sauté bread crumbs in ¼ cup butter until browned. Sprinkle over tomatoes. Bake at 325 for 20 minutes.

Ann Kobs
Pewaukee, WI

Stuffed Tomatoes

6 medium tomatoes
Salt
½ T. finely chopped onion
2 T. butter
½ cup chopped chicken or veal
½ cup bread crumbs
Pepper
1 egg, beaten
Cracker crumbs

Cut off top of tomatoes. Remove pulp; reserve. Salt tomato cavities; invert for 30 minutes. Add onion to butter; sauté 5 minutes. Add chicken or veal, bread crumbs, tomato pulp, salt and pepper; cook for 5 minutes. Add egg; cook one minute. Fill tomatoes with mixture; sprinkle with cracker crumbs. Bake in buttered pan 20 minutes.

Mary Perkins-Clemons
Bloomington, IN

Sun Stuffed Peppers

⅓ cup cooked brown rice
4 green peppers
¼ lb. ground beef
2 T. chopped onion
¼ cup chopped celery
¼ tsp. garlic powder
¼ tsp. dried basil
8-oz. can tomato sauce
½ cup raw sunflower seeds

Cut off pepper tops; remove seeds and membranes. Brown ground beef and onions. Add celery, garlic powder, basil and half the tomato sauce. Combine rice and sunflower seeds; add to mixture. Stuff green peppers lightly with mixture. Stand upright in 8 x 8 x 2-inch baking dish. Pour remaining tomato sauce over green peppers. Bake, covered at 350 degrees for 30 minutes. Uncover, bake for 5 minutes.

Joyce Wipf
Hurley, SD

Stuffed Tomatoes

Fiesta Corn Casserole

4 slices bacon
1 cup chopped onion
½ cup chopped sweet red peppers
½ cup chopped sweet green peppers
Optional: ½ jalapeño pepper, chopped
2 cups cream style corn
2 cups kernel corn
2 large eggs, lightly beaten
1 tsp. crumbled thyme
1 tsp. salt
½ tsp. pepper
¾ cup bread crumbs

Brown bacon until crisp. Remove; drain on paper towels. Sauté onions and peppers in 1 tablespoon bacon drippings. Mix cream corn, kernel corn, eggs, thyme, salt and pepper. Add bread crumbs, sautéed onions and peppers. Pour into 2 quart casserole dish. Bake at 350 degrees for 45-60 minutes.

Warren Dankert
Michigan City, IN

Cajun Cabbage

2 T. oil
1 small head cabbage, chopped
1 onion, chopped
1 lb. polish sausage, sliced
2 T. Cajun seasoning
½ cup water
½ cup vinegar
1 can Ro-tel tomatoes
2 T. sugar

Mix all ingredients in large pot. Simmer until cabbage is done.

Rose Martin
Wright, AR

Stuffed Zucchini

1 large zucchini, halved lengthwise
1 cup bread crumbs
2 cloves garlic, crushed
1/3 cup olive oil
2 medium onions, diced
1/4 cup pine nuts
2 T. raisins
2 T. chopped parsley
1 bunch scallions, diced
4 tomatoes, diced
Salt
Freshly ground pepper
Pinch cayenne pepper
1 cup water
Paprika

Remove some pulp from zucchini halves, leaving enough to have strong shell to hold filling. Chop removed pulp; mix in large bowl with all other ingredients. Stuff zucchini with mixture. Wrap tightly in aluminum foil. Place wrapped zucchini medium heat for 1/2 hour, or until tender. Unwrap top of foil; sprinkle with paprika. Cook 10 more minutes.

Evelyn Darer
New York, NY

Quickie Stuffed Peppers

4 medium green peppers
1/2 lb. lean ground beef
1 cup cooked rice
1 1/4 tsp. salt
1 egg, slightly beaten
2 T. minced onion
1 can tomato soup, undiluted
1/4 cup grated American cheese

Remove tops and seeds from peppers. Blanch peppers 10 minutes in hot water or until tender. Drain; place upright in 1 1/2 quart casserole. Combine ground beef, rice, salt, egg, onion and 1/2 cup tomato soup. Mix well. Fill peppers with meat mixture. Bake at 350 degrees for 30 minutes. Pour remainder of soup over peppers. Sprinkle with cheese; bake 15 minutes longer.

Dorris Medlin
Annandale, VA

main dishes

Michelle's Jam-Packed Meatballs

1 stalk celery

1 carrot

2 scallions

¼ cup mushrooms

2 slices whole grain bread, stale, crumbled

½ cup Quaker oats

1 ½ tsp. Italian seasoning

2 cloves garlic, minced

½ tsp. black pepper and red pepper blend

½ tsp. marjoram

½ tsp. basil

½ cup grated Parmesan/Romano cheese blend

1 lb. ground beef

1 egg yolk

¼ cup milk

½ cup prepared bulgur

In food processor, finely chop together celery, carrot, scallions and mushrooms. In large mixing bowl, combine bread crumbs, oats, Italian seasoning, garlic, pepper blend, marjoram, basil and cheese. Combine using your hands. Add meat, egg, milk and mixture from processor; combine thoroughly using hands. Add bulgur; mix. Using teaspoon, form into balls. Place on baking sheet. Bake at 350 degrees for 30 minutes. Add to your favorite sauce; heat. Serve over noodles or spoon into subs and top with grated provolone.

Michelle A. Jester
Parma, OH

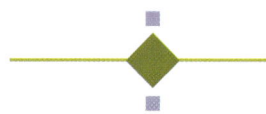

desserts

Apple Tort

Apple Tort

TORT:

¼ lb. butter, melted

1 cup sugar

2 eggs

2 tsp. vanilla

1 ¾ cups flour

2 tsp. baking powder

8-10 large apples, peeled, cut into eighths

Cinnamon

TOPPING:

¼ lb. butter

1 cup sugar

2 eggs

Cinnamon

Mix ¼ pound butter and 1 cup sugar; beat well. Add 2 eggs and vanilla; mix thoroughly. Combine flour and baking powder. Add to egg mixture; beat well. Spread on bottom of 9 or 10-inch springform pan. Stand apples on end in batter. Sprinkle with cinnamon. Bake at 350 degrees for 1 hour.

To prepare topping, cream together ¼ pound butter and 1 cup sugar. Add 2 eggs, sprinkle with cinnamon. Pour over tort. Lower heat to 325 degrees and bake for 20-25 minutes more. Serve warm with whipped cream topping over vanilla ice cream.

Marybeth Schilling
Valley Stream, NY

Baked Apples

6 tart apples, cored, pared half-way down

2 T. flour

3 T. butter, melted

½ cup brown sugar

½ tsp. vanilla

Place apples in baking dish with pared side up. Combine flour and butter. Add brown sugar and vanilla; stir. Spread mixture over apples. Bake at 425 degrees for 10 minutes; until crust is set. Lower temperature to 350 degrees. Bake about 30 minutes or until tender.

Kerrie Ann Skuran
Schaumburg, IL

New England Apple Roll

CRUST:

1 ¼ cups flour

½ cup sour cream

½ cup butter, softened

FILLING:

¼ cup maple syrup

¼ cup milk

¼ cup butter

2 T. sugar

2 T. brown sugar

2 medium apples, peeled, sliced

1 ½ T. cornstarch

½ cup raisins

½ tsp. vanilla

½ cup chopped walnuts

Simmer syrup, milk, butter, sugar, brown sugar, apples, cornstarch and raisins 10-15 minutes, until raisins are tender. Add vanilla and nuts; cool.

To prepare crust, combine all crust ingredients. Roll out dough to 15 x 10-inch rectangle.

Spread filling over dough. Roll up jellyroll fashion; seal edges. Place on greased cookie sheet. Bake at 425 degrees for 25 minutes, until golden brown. Cool 5 minutes; remove from pan. Slice when cooled.

Irene Gaige
Battle Mountain, NV

Red Apple Cobbler

1 ½ cups flour
2 tsp. baking powder
½ tsp. salt
1 cup sugar
1 egg, beaten
3 T. margarine, melted
1 cup milk

6-7 cooking apples
Juice of 1 lemon
(or ½ cup lemon concentrate)
½ tsp. vanilla extract
½ cup red cinnamon candies
1 cup sugar
1 cup water

In large bowl, mix together flour, baking powder, salt and 1 cup sugar. In separate bowl, combine egg, margarine and milk. Stir into flour mixture until well combined. Pour into 9 x 13-inch greased pan. Combine apples, lemon juice and vanilla; spread evenly over batter. Sprinkle red cinnamon candies evenly over apples. Combine 1 cup sugar with water; pour over fruit. Bake at 375 degrees for 50 minutes.

Lois Mason
Allegan, MI

Chocolate Carrot Cake

1 ½ cups sugar
1 cup oil
½ cup orange juice
4 eggs
1 tsp. vanilla
2 cups shredded carrots
4 oz. coconut
2 cups flour

¼ cup powdered cocoa
¼ cup powdered sugar
2 tsp. baking soda
1 tsp. salt
1 tsp. cinnamon
Powdered sugar

Grease and flour 10-inch Bundt pan. Combine sugar, oil, orange juice, eggs, vanilla, carrots and coconut. In separate bowl, sift together dry ingredients. Gradually mix dry ingredients into batter; pour into pan. Bake at 350 degrees for 50-55 minutes. Dust with powdered sugar.

Rachel Nydan
Northbridge, MA

Blueberry Soufflé

4 cups fresh blueberries, rinsed, drained
½ cup water
2 pkg. unflavored gelatin
½ cup pineapple juice
½ cup sugar
4 eggs, separated
1 cup heavy whipping cream
Additional blueberries for garnish

In saucepan, combine 2 cups blueberries and water. Simmer for 10 minutes; press mixture through a strainer. In large bowl, mix gelatin and pineapple juice. Stir in blueberry puree and sugar, until sugar is dissolved. Beat in egg yolks. Chill until mixture is syrupy. Fold in heavy cream. Beat egg whites until stiff and glossy. Fold in blueberry mixture and additional 2 cups of blueberries. Make aluminum foil collar around outer edge of 1-quart soufflé dish. Pour mixture into dish; chill until firm. Carefully remove foil collar. Decorate top of soufflé with rosettes of whipped cream, blueberries and some tiny leaves.

Ms. Edythe H. Boisvert
Amesbury, MA

Green Tomato Pie

3 cups sliced green tomatoes
2 cups chopped apples
1 cup raisins, soaked in hot water
⅔ cup brown sugar
½ tsp. cinnamon
⅓ cup sugar
2 T. butter
3 T. flour
Unbaked pie crust

Mix all ingredients together. Pour into pie crust. Bake at 425 degrees for 60 minutes.

Roger King
Elkhart, IN

Pumpkin Brownies

Pumpkin Brownies

1 cup flour
¼ cup instant mashed potatoes
1 tsp. baking powder
½ tsp. salt
1 tsp. cinnamon
½ cup margarine, melted
1 ½ cups sugar
1 egg
¾ cup canned pumpkin
½ cup chopped pecans

Sift dry ingredients. In separate bowl, stir together margarine, sugar, egg and pumpkin. Add dry ingredients and nuts. Stir until well blended. Pour into greased 9-inch square pan. Bake at 350 degrees for 40 minutes. Frost with cream cheese frosting or sprinkle powdered sugar for less fat.

Sabrina McCarthy
St. Marys, KS

Squash Pie

1 ½ cups cooked, strained squash
1 rounded T. flour
1 rounded tsp. cinnamon
1 rounded tsp. ginger
1 rounded tsp. cloves
1 rounded tsp. salt
½ heaping cup sugar
2 eggs, beaten
1 ½ cups milk
Pie shell, frozen, unbaked

Mix flour into squash. Add spices, salt and sugar; mix well. Add eggs and milk; mix well. Pour into pie shell. Bake at 450 degrees for 10 minutes. Reduce oven to 350 degrees. Bake until firm, about 40 minutes.

Jane Wilson
Oakland, CA

Harvest Pumpkin Cobbler

FILLING:

2 eggs, lightly beaten

1 cup evaporated milk

3 cups cooked, mashed, pumpkin

¾ cup sugar

½ cup brown sugar

1 T. flour

1 tsp. ground cinnamon

¼ tsp. ground ginger

¼ tsp. ground cloves

¼ tsp. ground nutmeg

¼ tsp. salt

CRUST:

½ cup butter

1 cup flour

1 cup sugar

1 T. baking powder

¼ tsp. salt

1 cup milk

1 tsp. vanilla

Optional: pecan halves

In bowl, combine eggs, evaporated milk and pumpkin. Add ¾ cup sugar, brown sugar, 1 tablespoon flour, cinnamon, ginger, cloves, nutmeg and ¼ teaspoon salt; beat lightly just until combined. Set aside.

Heat oven to 350 degrees. In 3-quart rectangular baking dish, melt butter in oven. In bowl, combine 1 cup flour, 1 cup sugar, baking powder, ¼ teaspoon salt, 1 cup milk and vanilla. Pour mixture over melted butter. Pour pumpkin mixture evenly over crust. Return to oven. Bake 50-55 minutes. Serve warm. Garnish with chopped nuts sprinkled on top.

Donna Rohwedder
Teutopoplis, IL

Cream Cheese Rhubarb Pie

¼ cup cornstarch

¾ cup sugar

Pinch of salt

½ cup water

1 T. lemon juice

3 rounded cups sliced rhubarb

9-inch unbaked pie shell

CREAM CHEESE TOPPING:

8-oz. pkg. cream cheese, softened

2 eggs

½ cup sugar

STREUSEL TOPPING:

⅓ cup oatmeal

½ cup packed brown sugar

2 T. flour

2 tsp. cinnamon

2 T. oleo, melted

⅓ cup nuts

In saucepan combine cornstarch, ¾ cup sugar, salt, water and lemon juice. Mix; add rhubarb. Cook; stirring often until mixture boils and thickens. Pour into pie shell. Bake at 425 degrees for 10 minutes. Beat cream cheese, eggs and sugar until smooth. Pour over pie. Combine streusel ingredients; sprinkle streusel topping over pie. Return to oven. Reduce heat to 325 degrees; bake for 35 minutes or until set.

Darla Birrell
Girard, PA

Chocolate Zucchini Cake

½ cup butter
½ cup cooking oil
1 ¾ cups sugar
2 eggs
2 tsp. vanilla
½ cup sour milk

2 ½ cups unsifted flour
4 T. cocoa
½ tsp. baking powder
2 tsp. baking soda
½ tsp. cinnamon
½ tsp. cloves
½ tsp. salt
2 cups grated zucchini
¼ cup chocolate chips

Cream together butter, oil and sugar. Add eggs, vanilla and sour milk. Mix together dry ingredients; add to creamed mixture. Stir in zucchini and chocolate chips. Bake in greased 9 x 13-inch pan at 350 degrees for 45-50 minutes.

Grant Anderson
Neillsville, WI

Diane Schmitt's Zucchini Pie

9-inch pie crust
1 cup milnot
1 cup sugar
1 egg
1 tsp. vanilla
2 T. flour
½ T. butter, melted
1 cup shredded zucchini
Cinnamon

Whisk together milnot, sugar, egg, vanilla, flour and butter. Add zucchini. Pour into pie shell and sprinkle cinnamon on top. Bake at 450 degrees for 15 minutes. Reduce oven temperature to 350 degrees; bake for 35 minutes.

Dana Schmitt
Greenfield, IN

Chocolate Zucchini Cake

Fresh Strawberry Pie

Juice of 1 lemon
1 can condensed milk
3 cups sliced strawberries
9-oz. container Cool Whip
1 pie shell, baked

Combine lemon juice, condensed milk and strawberries. Fold in Cool Whip; pour into pie shell. Refrigerate overnight.

Ira Broxson
Merryville, LA

Strawberry Pie

1 cup sugar

3 T. cornstarch

1 cup water

2 T. white Karo syrup

¼ cup strawberry Jello-O mix

1 qt. fresh strawberries

9-inch pie shell, baked

Mix sugar, cornstarch, water and syrup. Heat until thick and clear. Mix in Jell-O; cool. Place strawberries in pie crust. Pour mixture on top. Chill 2 hours in refrigerator. Serve with whipped cream.

Becky Gilson
Austin, MN

Mamie Eisenhower's Pumpkin Chiffon Pie

1 pkg. unflavored gelatin

¾ cup light brown sugar

½ tsp. cinnamon

½ tsp. nutmeg

¾ cup milk

3 eggs, separated

1 ½ cups cooked pumpkin

½ cup sugar

9-inch pie shell, baked

Mix gelatin, brown sugar, cinnamon and nutmeg together in double boiler. Stir in milk. Beat in egg yolks, then pumpkin. Place over boiling water and cook, stirring often until mixture is heated through. Remove from heat; chill until mixture begins to set. Beat egg whites stiff, but not dry. Gradually beat in sugar until very stiff. Fold pumpkin mixture into egg whites. Pour into pie shell. Chill until firm; garnish with whipped cream.

Anita Mills
Wichita Falls, TX

Pumpkin Cream Cheese Muffins

MUFFIN:
2 cups sugar
2 ¼ cups flour
2 tsp. baking powder
2 tsp. cinnamon
½ tsp. salt
¼ tsp. baking soda
2 eggs
1 ¼ cups pumpkin
¼ cup oil
1 tsp. vanilla

FILLING:
8-oz. cream cheese
1 egg
2 T. sugar

CRUMB TOPPING:
4 T. flour
4 T. sugar
½ tsp. cinnamon
2 T. butter

To prepare muffins, mix together dry ingredients. In separate bowl mix wet ingredients. Combine wet and dry ingredients until just moistened.

To prepare filling, mix all ingredients; set aside.

To prepare topping, mix flour, sugar and cinnamon. Cut in butter.

To assemble, line muffin tins with paper cups. Fill cups half full of muffin mixture. Add 1 teaspoon of filling in center of muffin mixture, being careful not to get too close to edge. Sprinkle crumbs on top. Bake at 375 degrees for 20-25 minutes.

Barbara Pomaville
Pinconning, MI

Magic Blueberry Cobbler

2 cups fresh blueberries
2 tsp. cornstarch
2 cups sugar
1/8 cup water
1 cup flour
1 1/2 tsp. baking powder
Dash of salt
3/4 cup milk
1/4 lb. oleo, melted

Combine blueberries, cornstarch, 1 cup sugar and water in saucepan over medium heat. Heat to boiling; set aside. Mix 1/2 cup sugar, flour, baking powder, salt and milk in bowl. Pour oleo in 9 x 13-inch cake pan. Add dry ingredients. Pour in blueberry mixture. Do not stir. Sprinkle 1/2 cup sugar. Bake at 350 degrees for 30-40 minutes.

Mary Gonce
Fairview, TN

Rhubarb Pudding

4 cups chopped rhubarb
1 3/4 cups sugar
3 T. butter
1 cup flour
1/4 tsp. salt
1 tsp. baking powder
1/2 cup milk
1 T. cornstarch
1/4 tsp. salt
1 cup hot water

Grease 8 x 8-inch pan. Pour rhubarb into pan. Cream together 3/4 cup sugar and butter. Sift together flour, salt and baking powder. Add sifted ingredients and milk to creamed mixture. Pour over rhubarb. Mix together 1 cup sugar, cornstarch and salt. Sprinkle on top. Pour hot water over entire mixture. Bake at 350 degrees until done.

Marie Loskill
Plano, IL

Cranberry Orange Cake

Cranberry Orange Cake

2 ¼ cups flour

1 tsp. baking powder

1 tsp. soda

¼ tsp. salt

1 cup chopped walnuts

1 cup chopped pitted dates

2 eggs, beaten

1 cup sugar

¾ cup salad oil

1 cup buttermilk

1 cup coarsely chopped fresh cranberries

Grated peel of 2 oranges

¼ cup orange juice

¼ cup sugar

Sift dry ingredients; add walnuts and dates. Mix well; set aside. Combine eggs, sugar, oil, buttermilk, cranberries, and orange peel. Mix well. Add dry ingredients gradually. Mix until smooth after each addition. Spoon into greased 9-inch tube pan. Bake at 350 degrees for 1 hour. Remove; place on wire rack. Do not remove from pan. Combine orange juice and sugar. Mix well. Pour gradually over cake. Juice should soak into cake. When cool, place in refrigerator for 24 hours before removing from pan.

Dorris Medlin
Annandale, VA

Mashed Potato Cake

3 eggs
1 cup brown sugar
1 cup sugar
2/3 cup shortening
1 cup mashed potatoes
2 cups milk
1/4 cup cocoa
2 cups flour
1/2 tsp. cinnamon
1/2 tsp. nutmeg
1 1/2 tsp. baking powder
1 1/2 tsp. baking soda

Mix eggs and sugars. Add shortening and potatoes; mix well. Stir in milk. Mix cocoa, flour, cinnamon, nutmeg, baking powder and baking soda. Add to mix. Pour in greased and floured 9 x 13-inch pan. Bake at 350 degrees for 50 minutes.

Tresa Evans
Altamont, IL

Peach Custard Pie

2 cups milk
2 eggs
3 T. cornstarch
Dash of salt
1 tsp. vanilla
1 T. butter
4-6 fresh peaches, peeled, sliced
8-inch ready-made graham cracker crust
Optional: whipped cream

Combine milk, eggs, cornstarch and salt in saucepan. Cook over medium heat, constantly stirring, until mixture boils and starts to thicken. Remove from heat, add vanilla and butter; mix well. Set aside to cool. Arrange peach slices in crust. Pour cooled custard mixture over peaches. Cover with whipped cream; store in refrigerator until set.

Vivian Nikanow
Chicago, IL

desserts

Carrot Cake with Butter Cream Frosting

CAKE:

2 cups grated carrots

2 T. lemon juice

1 cup crushed, drained pineapple

1 cup raisins

1 cup chopped walnuts

½ cup honey

1 ½ cups flour

1 cup sugar

1 tsp. baking soda

1 tsp. baking powder

1 tsp. salt

1 tsp. cinnamon

½ tsp. cloves

½ tsp. allspice

½ tsp. ginger

½ tsp. nutmeg

3 eggs

BUTTER CREAM FROSTING:

¼ cup butter, melted

¼ cup sweet cream

1 tsp. vanilla

3 cups powdered sugar

To prepare cake, mix carrots, lemon juice, pineapple, raisins, walnuts and honey. In separate bowl combine flour, sugar, baking soda, baking powder, salt, cinnamon, cloves, allspice, ginger and nutmeg. Add eggs; mix well. Add carrot mixture; beat until combined. Grease Bundt or loaf pan; pour batter into pan. Bake at 350 degrees for 1-1 1/2 hours. Remove, turn out and let cool on wire rack.

To prepare frosting, mix butter, cream and vanilla together in bowl. Slowly beat in powdered sugar until thick and creamy. Frost cake; serve.

Scott Zak
Boston, MA

Walnut Carrot Cake

1 1/2 cups black walnuts
3 cups sifted flour
3 tsp. baking powder
1 tsp. salt
2 cups firmly packed brown sugar
4 large eggs
1 cup oil
1 1/2 tsp. cinnamon
1 tsp. nutmeg
1/4 tsp. cloves
3 T. milk
3 cups grated carrots

Finely chop 1/2 cup walnuts. Grease three 9-inch layer cake pans. Sprinkle each pan with 2 1/2 tablespoons walnuts. Chop remaining nuts more coarsely; set aside. Resift flour with baking powder and salt. Combine brown sugar, eggs, oil and spices. Beat at high speed until well mixed. Add half of flour mixture; stir until well blended. Add milk and remaining flour. Stir in carrots and chopped nuts. Divide batter evenly in pans. Bake at 350 degrees for 25 minutes. Let stand in pans on wire rack for 10 minutes. Turn cakes out onto wire rack. When cool, frost with butter cream frosting. Decorate with walnut halves.

Ola Harmon
Shelby, NC

Rhubarb Crunch

Rhubarb, chopped

THICKENING:

1 cup sugar
2 T. cornstarch
1 cup water
1 tsp. vanilla

CRUST:

1 cup flour
3/4 cup oatmeal
1 cup brown sugar
1 tsp. cinnamon
1/3 cup margarine

Combine thickening ingredients; cook until thick and clear. Mix together crust ingredients until crumbly. Line bottom of 9 x 13-inch pan with crust dough; reserving some for topping. Place rhubarb over crust. Spread thickening evenly over rhubarb. Sprinkle remaining crust mixture on top. Bake at 350 degrees for 1 hour.

Debra Burns
Palo, MI

Walnut Carrot Cake

Apple Nut Cake

2 cups sugar

3 eggs

1 1/2 cups oil

1/2 cup orange juice

1 tsp. vanilla

3 cups flour

1 1/2 tsp. salt

1 1/2 tsp. cinnamon

1 1/2 tsp. baking soda

1 cup grated apple

1 cup coconut

1 cup chopped nuts

ICING:

1 stick margarine

1 cup sugar

1/2 tsp. baking soda

1/2 cup buttermilk

Mix sugar, eggs and oil. Add orange juice and vanilla. Sift dry ingredients together; add to mix. Add apple, coconut and nuts; mix well. Bake at 325 degrees for 1 1/2 hours.

To prepare icing, melt margarine; add sugar, baking soda and buttermilk. Heat to boiling. Turn off heat; let cool. Pour sauce over cake; let stand for 1 hour before removing cake from pan.

Mary Ann Dunphy
Dallas, GA

Apple and Pecan Cake

1 egg, beaten

1/2 cup flour

1/2 tsp. cinnamon

1 tsp. vanilla

3/4 cup firmly packed brown sugar

1/2 tsp. salt

1/2 tsp. baking soda

1 cup peeled, chopped, tart apples

1 cup coarsely chopped pecans

In medium bowl, mix egg, flour, cinnamon, vanilla, brown sugar, salt and baking soda. Fold apples and pecans into mixture. Turn into greased 8-inch pie plate. Bake at 350 degrees for 25 minutes. Serve with vanilla ice cream or whipped cream.

Jenny Robinson
Arnold, MD

desserts

Apple Cranberry Crunch

BATTER:
6 baking apples, peeled, cored, chopped
1 can whole berry cranberry sauce
¼ cup honey

TOPPING:
1 cup quick oats
½ cup flour
½ cup brown sugar
1 tsp. nutmeg
1 T. cinnamon
½ stick margarine, melted

To prepare batter, mix all ingredients. Pour into baking dish. In separate bowl, mix first 5 topping ingredients; spread over apple mixture. Drizzle margarine on top. Bake at 350 degrees for 45 minutes.

Hal Wenig
Flushing, NY

Irma Jane's Applesauce Cake

1 cup vegetable oil
2 cups sugar
2 cups applesauce
2 tsp. allspice
2 tsp. nutmeg
2 tsp. cloves
2 tsp. cinnamon
3 ½ cups flour
1 box raisins
2 cups walnuts

Mix oil and sugar together; stir in applesauce. Add remaining ingredients; mix thoroughly. Pour into greased Bundt pan. Bake at 325 degrees for 1 hour. Cool 15 minutes; remove from pan.

Mr. Todd Carey
Mechanicsville, VA

Pumpkin Walnut Cheesecake

Pumpkin Walnut Cheesecake

CHEESECAKE:

6-oz. box zwieback crackers, crushed

¼ cup sugar

6 T. butter, melted

3 (8-oz.) pkg. cream cheese, softened, room temperature

¾ cup sugar

¾ cup firmly packed brown sugar

5 eggs

1 lb. can pumpkin

1 tsp. ground cinnamon

½ tsp. ground nutmeg

¼ tsp. ground cloves

¼ cup heavy cream

WALNUT TOPPING:

6 T. butter

1 cup firmly packed light brown sugar

1 cup coarsely chopped walnuts

Combine crackers, sugar and melted butter in bowl. Press firmly into bottom of 9-inch springform pan. Chill briefly. Beat cream cheese with electric mixer until smooth. Add sugars gradually; beating until just light and fluffy. Add eggs, one at a time. Beat well after each addition. Beat in pumpkin, cinnamon, nutmeg, cloves and heavy cream at low speed. Pour into prepared pan. Bake at 350 degrees for 1 hour and 35 minutes.

To prepare walnut topping, beat butter with brown sugar in small bowl. Stir in walnuts.

Carefully remove cake from oven; spoon on walnut topping; bake additional 10 minutes. Remove cake from oven; let cool completely. Refrigerate several hours. Serve at room temperature.

Jean Fields
Apple Valley, CA

Best Rhubarb Shortcake

4 cups cubed rhubarb
1 ¾ cups sugar
3 T. butter
1 cup flour
1 tsp. baking powder
½ tsp. salt
½ cup milk
1 T. cornstarch
1 cup boiling water

Place rhubarb in 8 x 8-inch pan. Cream ¾ cup sugar and butter. Mix flour, baking powder and ¼ teaspoon salt. Add milk and flour mixture to creamed mixture. Spread over rhubarb. Combine 1 cup sugar, cornstarch and ¼ teaspoon salt. Sprinkle on top. Pour boiling water over top. Bake at 350 degrees for 1 hour.

Mary Spoonholtz
Eau Claire, MI

Loaded Apple Pie

1 stick butter, melted
½ cup sugar
½ cup brown sugar
7 medium red delicious apples, peeled, cored, sliced
¼ cup rum
Cinnamon
Nutmeg
Pie Shell
Sugar

In heated skillet, cook butter, sugar and brown sugar until golden. Add apples, rum, cinnamon and nutmeg. Heat until apples are half-cooked. Place mixture in pie shell. Add top crust; crimp edges. Slice small holes in top. Sprinkle with sugar. Bake at 400 degrees for 30 minutes.

Thomas Boyer
Coldspring, TX

Rhubarb Cake

½ cup shortening

1 ½ cups sugar

1 egg

1 tsp. vanilla

½ cup sour cream

½ cup buttermilk

2 cups flour

2 cups chopped rhubarb

1 tsp. baking soda

1 tsp. salt

½ cup nuts

TOPPING:

1 tsp. cinnamon

½ cup brown sugar

Cream shortening and sugar. Add egg, vanilla, sour cream and buttermilk. Sprinkle ¼ cup flour over rhubarb. Sift remaining flour with baking soda and salt. Add sifted mixture, rhubarb and nuts to creamed mixture. Pour into 9 x 13-inch pan. Combine topping ingredients and sprinkle over batter. Bake at 350 degrees for 40 minutes.

Elsie McGlughy
Omaha, NE

Blueberry Cake

½ cup butter

1 cup sugar

2 eggs, separated, beaten

1 tsp. vanilla

1 ½ cups flour

1 tsp. baking powder

½ cup milk

1 ½ cups blueberries or huckleberries

Powdered sugar

Cream butter and sugar. Add egg yolks and vanilla. Sift dry ingredients together; add alternately with milk to creamed mixture. Beat well after each addition. Fold in stiffly beaten egg whites. Pour half batter into greased 8 or 9-inch square pan. Cover with berries. Pour remaining batter over berries. Bake at 350 degrees for 35 minutes. Cool 15 minutes, sprinkle powdered sugar over cake.

Debra Burns
Palo, MI

Zucchini Crisp

FILLING:

8 cups peeled, seeded, thinly sliced zucchini

2/3 cup lemon juice

1 cup sugar

1 tsp. cinnamon

1/4 tsp. nutmeg

1 cup shredded coconut

1/2 cup butter

CRUST:

1 cup flour

6 T. butter

1/2 cup sugar

Dash salt

1 tsp. cinnamon

1 cup chopped pecans

To prepare filling, combine zucchini and lemon juice. Cook until tender about 30-40 minutes. During last 10 minutes of cooking, add remaining filling ingredients. Mix well; continue cooking.

To prepare crust, combine all ingredients, except nuts, with pastry blender. Remove 1/2 cup crust mixture; add to cooked zucchini mixture. Add nuts to remaining crust mixture.

Pour filling into lightly greased 9 x 13-inch pan. Sprinkle crust/nut mixture on top. Bake at 375 degrees for 30 minutes. Serve warm with whipped topping or ice cream.

Mrs. P. Karenbauer
Butler, PA

Chocolate Chip Orange Crunchies

1 cup shortening
½ tsp. salt
1 T. grated orange rind
2 T. orange juice
⅔ cup firmly packed brown sugar
1 egg
2 cups flour
¼ tsp. baking soda
¾ cup chopped nuts
1 cup chocolate chips

Blend shortening, salt, orange rind and orange juice. Add brown sugar gradually, cream well. Add egg; beat. Sift flour with baking soda; add to creamed mixture. Blend. Add nuts and chocolate chips; mix well. Drop by tablespoons full onto greased baking sheet; flatten. Bake at 375 degrees for 12-15 minutes.

Edgar and Marjorie Evans
Irvine, CA

Lemon Zucchini Cookies

BATTER:

2 cups flour
1 tsp. baking powder
¾ cup butter, softened
¾ cup sugar
1 egg, beaten
1 tsp. grated lemon zest
1-1 ½ cups unpeeled, shredded zucchini
Optional: 1 cup walnuts or pecans

FROSTING:

1 cup powdered sugar
1 ½ T. lemon juice

To prepare batter, mix together flour and baking powder. Cream butter and sugar. Beat egg and lemon zest until fluffy. Fold in dry ingredients. Stir in zucchini and nuts. Drop teaspoon size on greased cookie sheet. Bake at 375 degrees for 15-20 minutes. Place on cooling rack.

To prepare frosting, combine powdered sugar and lemon juice. Drizzle over cooled cookies.

Babette A. Clapper
Floyd, NY

Index

A

alfalfa sprouts
    Tuna Delights, 9
Aloo Ghobi, 74
Ann's Party Spinach, 121
apples
    Apple and Pecan Cake, 148
    Apple Cranberry Crunch, 149
    Apple Nut Cake, 148
    Apple Tort, 128
    Baked Apples, 128
    Green Tomato Pie, 131
    Loaded Apple Pie, 152
    New England Apple Roll, 129
    Red Apple Cobbler, 130
    Zucchini Apple Bread, 69
Apple and Pecan Cake, 148
Apple Cranberry Crunch, 149
Apple Nut Cake, 148
Apple Tort, 128
artichokes
    Ann's Party Spinach, 121
    Hot Artichoke Dip, 23
    Vegetable Antipasto, 81
asparagus
    Beef Negamaki Rolls, 8
    Pickled Homegrown Garlic, Beans or Asparagus, 30
avocado
    Avocado and Tomato Salad with Basil Vinaigrette, 41
    Beef Negamaki Rolls, 8
    Lake Charles Dip, 20
    Pueblo Wrap, 115
    Southwestern Caesar Salad, 44
Avocado and Tomato Salad with Basil Vinaigrette, 41

B

Baked Apples, 128
bananas
    Black Bean Burgers with Banana Ketchup, 120
basil
    Avocado and Tomato Salad with Basil Vinaigrette, 41
    Black Bean Burgers with Banana Ketchup, 120
    Eggplant Italiano, 118
    Garden Macaroni Salad, 43
    Garden Minestrone Soup, 56
    Herb Salt, 33
    La Ratatouille Nicoise, 121
    Mexican Vegetable Lasagna, 106
    Michelle's Jam-Packed Meatballs, 126
    Parsley Pesto, 25
    Pasta Fazool, 96
    Savory Herb and Bleu Cheesecake, 14
    Shrimp Fettuccine with Sun-Dried Tomatoes, 79
    Summer Pasta Salad, 46
    Summer Pasta with Fresh Tomatoes and Herbs, 77
    Sun Stuffed Peppers, 122
    Tomato Pie, 112
    Tomatoes Stuffed with Antipasto Salad, 84
    Vegetable Antipasto, 81
    White Clam Sauce, 35
    Zucchini Crescent Bake, 82
bay leaf
    Chicken and Rice Soup, 60
    Spaghetti Sauce, 27
    Split Pea Soup, 51
    Tomato Soup, 62

beans
    Beef Negamaki Rolls, 8
    Chicken Pot Pie, 108
    Garden Minestrone Soup, 56
    Hamburger Pie, 103
    Italian Salad, 74
    Pasta Fazool, 96
    Pickled Homegrown Garlic, Beans or Asparagus, 30
    Southern France Green Beans, 80
    Stephanie's Garden Vegetable Soup, 58
beef
    Beef Negamaki Rolls, 8
    Chunky Mushroom Chili, 58
    Cody's Soup, 55
    Cornish Pasties, 105
    Country Goulash, 98
    Hamburger Pie, 103
    Michelle's Jam-Packed Meatballs, 126
    Micro Beef Tostada Pie, 99
    Pancit Noodles with Vegetables, 91
    Quickie Stuffed Peppers, 125
    Shipwreck, 94
    Stuffed Bell Peppers, 112
    Stuffed Cabbage Rolls, 116
    Stuffed Pumpkin, 105
    Sun Stuffed Peppers, 122
    Taco Dip, 23
    Vegetables and Rice, 95
    Zucchini Pizza, 119
Beef Negamaki Rolls, 8
beets
    Elegant Beet Salad, 38
Best Rhubarb Shortcake, 152
black beans
    Black Bean Burgers with Banana Ketchup, 120
    Pueblo Wrap, 115
    Southwestern 3 Bean and Corn Salsa, 18
Black Bean Burgers with Banana Ketchup, 120
blueberries
    Blueberry Cake, 153
    Blueberry Muffins, 72
    Blueberry Soufflé, 131
    Magic Blueberry Cobbler, 141
Blueberry Cake, 153
Blueberry Muffins, 72
Blueberry Soufflé, 131
Bread Machine Zucchini Bread, 67
broccoli
    Broccoli Salad, 44
    Italian Salad, 74
    Tri-Pasta Salad, 38
Broccoli Salad, 45
Bulgur
    Michelle's Jam-Packed Meatballs, 126
    Tabbouleh, 30

C

cabbage
    Cajun Cabbage, 124
    Country Goulash, 98
    Garden Delight, 94
    Garden Minestrone Soup, 56
    Stuffed Bell Peppers, 112
    Stuffed Cabbage Rolls, 116
    Vegetable Medley Soup, 60
    Vegetables and Rice, 95
Cajun Cabbage, 124
Caldo Verde, 55
Camille's Eggplant Casserole, 104
carrots
    Beef Negamaki Rolls, 8
    Carrot Cake with Butter Cream Frosting, 145
    Carrots with Balsamic Vinegar, 75
    Chicken À la Tom, 110
    Chicken and Rice Soup, 60
    Chicken Pot Pie, 108
    Chocolate Carrot Cake, 130
    Cornish Pasties, 105
    Garden Delight, 94
    Garden Loaf, 64
    Garden Minestrone Soup, 56
    Lemon-Dill Turkey Pitas, 113
    Marinated Carrot Salad, 43
    Marinated Carrots, 85
    Michelle's Jam-Packed Meatballs, 126
    Pasta Fazool, 96
    Piccadilly Cafeteria's Carrot Soufflé, 88
    Potato Leek Soup, 50
    Quick New England Chowder, 50
    Split Pea Soup, 51
    Squash Supreme, 87
    Stephanie's Garden Vegetable Soup, 58
    Vegetable and Cheese Chowder, 61
    Vegetable Antipasto, 81
    Vegetables and Rice, 95
    Walnut Carrot Cake, 146
    Zucchini Casserole, 107
Carrot Cake with Butter Cream Frosting, 145
Carrots with Balsamic Vinegar, 75
cauliflower
    Aloo Ghobi, 74
    Red and White Salad, 39
celery
    Chicken À la Tom, 110
    Chicken and Rice Soup, 60
    Chicken Breast in Sour Cream, 101
    Cody's Soup, 55
    Creole Chicken Pie, 117
    Elegant Beet Salad, 38
    Frozen Cucumbers, 15
    Garden Macaroni Salad, 43
    Garden Minestrone Soup, 56
    Lemon Celery Soup, 48
    Michelle's Jam-Packed Meatballs, 126
    Pasta Fazool, 96
    Potato Leek Soup, 50
    Quick New England Clam Chowder, 50
    Salad Dressing, 32
    Shrimp Mousse, 13
    Spaghetti Sauce, 27
    Spicy Hot Green Tomato Preserves, 26
    Split Pea Soup, 51
    Stephanie's Garden Vegetable Soup, 58
    Sun Stuffed Peppers, 122
    Tomato Soup, 62
    Vegetable and Cheese Chowder, 61
    Whole Stuffed Pumpkin with Sausage, 110
Cherry Nut Zucchini Bread, 68
chicken
    Chicken À la Tom, 110
    Chicken and Rice Soup, 60
    Chicken Breast in Sour Cream, 101
    Chicken Piccata, 98
    Chicken Pot Pie, 108
    Chicken Tarragon, 101
    Chicken Tortilla Soup, 48
    Chili-Cheese Chicken Soup with Rice, 53
    Creole Chicken Pie, 117
    Grilled Vegetables and Chicken Sandwich, 103
    Herbed Chicken Breast, 100
    Rosemary's Chicken, 90
    Stuffed Tomatoes, 122
Chicken À la Tom, 110
Chicken and Rice Soup, 60
Chicken Breast in Sour Cream, 101

156   index

Chicken Piccata, 98
Chicken Pot Pie, 108
Chicken Tarragon, 101
Chicken Tortilla Soup, 48
chickpeas
    Garden Minestrone Soup, 56
    Hail Hail for Kale Soup, 54
    Tomatoes Stuffed with Antipasto Salad, 84
Chili-Cheese Chicken Soup with Rice, 53
chives
    Green/Yellow Garden Wheel, 104
    Herbed Chicken Breast, 100
    Italian Salad, 74
    Savory Herb and Bleu Cheesecake, 14
    Sliced Baked Potatoes, 78
    Spinach Cheese Pie, 111
    Tomato Pie, 112
Chocolate Carrot Cake, 130
Chocolate Chip Orange Crunchies, 155
Chocolate Zucchini Cake, 136
Chunky Mushroom Chili, 58
cilantro
    Chicken Tortilla Soup, 48
    Chili-Cheese Chicken Soup with Rice, 53
    Fire-Roasted Tomato Chipotle Salsa, 19
    Northport Picante, 22
    Pueblo Wrap, 115
    Southwestern Caesar Salad, 44
    Southwestern 3 Bean and Corn Salsa, 18
clams
    Quick New England Clam Chowder, 50
    White Clam Sauce, 35
    Zucchini and Clam Casserole, 93
coconut
    Apple Nut Cake, 148
    Chocolate Carrot Cake, 130
    Mini-Chocolate Chip and Coconut Zucchini Loaves, 65
    Sweet Potato Casserole, 75
    Zucchini Crisp, 154
Cody's Soup, 55
collards
    Caldo Verde, 55
corn
    Chicken Pot Pie, 108
    Chicken Tortilla Soup, 48
    Corn Soufflé, 87
    Fiesta Corn Casserole, 124
    Fried Corn on the Cob, 79
    Southwestern 3 Bean and Corn Salsa, 18
    Stephanie's Garden Vegetable Soup, 58
    Vegetable Chili, 59
    Vegetable Medley Soup, 60
    Whole Stuffed Pumpkin with Sausage, 110
Corn Soufflé, 87
corned beef
    Corned Beef Dip, 18
Corned Beef Dip, 18
Cornish Pasties, 105
Country Goulash, 98
Cowboy Salad, 42
cranberries
    Cranberry Orange Cake, 143
Cranberry Orange Cake, 143
Cream Cheese Rhubarb Pie, 135
Creamy Cucumber Dressing, 34
Creole Chicken Pie, 117
cucumbers
    Creamy Cucumber Dressing, 34
    Frozen Cucumbers, 14
    Garden Macaroni Salad, 43
    Italian Salad, 74
    Summer Pasta Salad, 46
    Veggie Pasta Toss, 80
Curry Dip, 25

D
dates
    Cranberry Orange Cake, 143
Diane Schmitt's Zucchini Pie, 136
dill
    Creamy Cucumber Dressing, 34
    Herb Salt, 33
    Lemon-Dill Turkey Pitas, 113
    Marinated Carrot Salad, 43
    Pickled Homegrown Garlic, Beans or Asparagus, 30
    Tomato Pie, 112

E
eggplant
    Camille's Eggplant Casserole, 104
    Eggplant Italiano, 118
    Grilled Vegetables and Chicken Sandwich, 103
    La Ratatouille Nicoise, 121
    Mexican Eggplant, 118
    Mexican Vegetable Lasagna, 106
Eggplant Italiano, 118
Elegant Beet Salad, 38

F
Fiesta Corn Casserole, 124
Fire-Roasted Tomato Chipotle Salsa, 19
fish
    Lemon and Thyme Flounder, 108
    Pescado Fabiola, 99
Fresh Strawberry Pie, 138
Fried Corn on the Cob, 79
Frozen Cucumbers, 15

G
garbanzo beans
    Hummus, 35
    Southwestern 3 Bean and Corn Salsa, 18
Garden Delight, 94
Garden Loaf, 64
Garden Macaroni Salad, 43
Garden Minestrone Soup, 56
Garden Vegetable Pilaf, 85
garlic
    Aloo Ghobi, 74
    Avocado and Tomato Salad with Basil Vinaigrette, 41
    Black Bean Burgers with Banana Ketchup, 120
    Bread Machine Zucchini Bread, 67
    Caldo Verde, 55
    Chicken Tortilla Soup, 48
    Chili-Cheese Chicken Soup with Rice, 53
    Chunky Mushroom Chili, 58
    Cornish Pasties, 105
    Creole Chicken Pie, 117
    Eggplant Italiano, 118
    Fire-Roasted Tomato Chipotle Salsa, 19
    Garden Delight, 94
    Garden Minestrone Soup, 56
    Grilled Vegetables and Chicken Sandwich, 103
    Hail Hail for Kale Soup, 54
    Hummus, 35
    Italy's Peasant-Style Tomato Bread Soup, 49
    La Ratatouille Nicoise, 121
    Lemon Rice, 77
    Mexican Vegetable Lasagna, 106
    Michelle's Jam-Packed Meatballs, 126
    Mozzarella and Tomato Salad, 45
    Pancit Noodles with Vegetables, 91
    Parsley Pesto, 25
    Pasta Fazool, 96
    Pickled Homegrown Garlic, Beans or Asparagus, 30
    Pueblo Wrap, 115
    Rosemary's Chicken, 90
    Savory Herb and Bleu Cheesecake, 14
    Shrimp Fettuccine with Sun-Dried Tomatoes, 79
    Southern France Green Beans, 80
    Southwestern Caesar Salad, 44
    Spicy Hot Green Tomato Preserves, 26
    Split Pea Soup, 51
    Stuffed Pumpkin, 105
    Stuffed Zucchini, 125
    Summer Pasta with Fresh Tomatoes and Herbs, 77
    Tabbouleh, 30
    Vegetable Antipasto, 81
    Vegetable Herb Marinade, 20
    White Clam Sauce, 35
    Zucchini Country Style, 88
    Zucchini Soup, 51
German Potato Salad, 39
Gourmet Mint Butter, 28
Green Tomato Pickles, 26
Green Tomato Pie, 131
Green/Yellow Garden Wheel, 104
Grilled Vegetables and Chicken Sandwich, 103

H
Hail Hail for Kale Soup, 54
Hamburger Pie, 103
Harvest Pumpkin Cobbler, 134
Herb Salt, 33
Herbed Chicken Breast, 100
Herbed Shallots in Phyllo Purses, 16
Hot Artichoke Dip, 23
Hot Pepper Butter, 29
huckleberries
    Huckleberry Muffins, 71
Huckleberry Muffins, 71
Hummus, 35

I
Irma Jane's Applesauce Cake, 149
Italian Salad, 74
Italy's Peasant-Style Tomato Bread Soup, 49

J
Jani's Summer Salad, 42

K
kale
    Hail Hail for Kale Soup, 54
Kerrie Ann's 1000 Island Dressing, 36
kiwi
    Jani's Summer Salad, 42

L
La Ratatouille Nicoise, 121
Lake Charles Dip, 20
leeks
    Potato Leek Soup, 50
lemon
    Chicken Piccata, 98
    Curry Dip, 25
    Fresh Strawberry Pie, 138
    Garden Loaf, 64
    Hummus, 35
    Lake Charles Dip, 20
    Lemon Celery Soup, 48
    Lemon-Dill Turkey Pitas, 113
    Lemon Zucchini Cookies, 155

index   **157**

Red Apple Cobbler, 130
Southern France Green Beans, 80
Southwestern Caesar Salad, 44
Tabbouleh, 30
Vegetable Herb Marinade, 20
Zucchini Strawberry Jam, 27
Lemon and Thyme Flounder, 108
Lemon Celery Soup, 48
Lemon-Dill Turkey Pitas, 113
Lemon Rice, 77
Lemon Zucchini Cookies, 155
lettuce
- Jani's Summer Salad, 42
- Lemon-Dill Turkey Pitas, 113
- Pueblo Wrap, 115
- Southwestern Caesar Salad, 44

Loaded Apple Pie, 152

M

Magic Blueberry Cobbler, 141
Mamie Eisenhower's Pumpkin Chiffon Pie, 139
maraschino cherries
- Cherry Nut Zucchini Bread, 68

Marinated Carrot Salad, 43
Marinated Carrots, 85
marjoram
- Michelle's Jam-Packed Meatballs, 126

Marvelous Cole Slaw Dressing, 32
Mashed Potato Cake, 144
Mexican Eggplant, 118
Mexican Vegetable Lasagna, 106
Mexican Zucchini Bake, 100
Michelle's Jam-Packed Meatballs, 126
Micro Beef Tostada Pie, 99
Mini-Chocolate Chip and Coconut Zucchini Loaves, 65
mint
- Gourmet Mint Butter, 27

Mock Crab Cakes, 13
Mozzarella and Tomato Salad, 45
mushrooms
- Ann's Party Spinach, 121
- Chicken À la Tom, 110
- Chicken Breast in Sour Cream, 101
- Chicken Tarragon, 101
- Chunky Mushroom Chili, 58
- Garden Minestrone Soup, 56
- Mexican Zucchini Bake, 100
- Michelle's Jam-Packed Meatballs, 126
- Vegetable Antipasto, 81
- Zucchini Pizza, 119

N

New England Apple Roll, 129
Northport Picante, 22

O

okra
- Vegetable Medley Soup, 60

Old South Jambalaya, 96
onions
- Aloo Ghobi, 74
- Black Bean Burgers with Banana Ketchup, 120
- Broccoli Salad, 44
- Cajun Cabbage, 124
- Caldo Verde, 55
- Camille's Eggplant Casserole, 104
- Cornish Pasties, 105
- Chicken À la Tom, 110
- Chicken and Rice Soup, 60
- Chicken Breast in Sour Cream, 101
- Chicken Tarragon, 101
- Chicken Tortilla Soup, 48

Chili-Cheese Chicken Soup with Rice, 53
Chunky Mushroom Chili, 58
Cody's Soup, 55
Corned Beef Dip, 18
Country Goulash, 98
Cowboy Salad, 42
Creamy Cucumber Dressing, 34
Creole Chicken Pie, 117
Fiesta Corn Casserole, 124
Fire-Roasted Tomato Chipotle Salsa, 19
Frozen Cucumbers, 15
Garden Delight, 94
Garden Macaroni Salad, 43
Garden Minestrone Soup, 56
German Potato Salad, 39
Green Tomato Pickles, 26
Grilled Vegetables and Chicken Sandwich, 103
Hail Hail for Kale Soup, 54
Hamburger Pie, 103
Italian Salad, 74
Italy's Peasant-Style Tomato Bread Soup, 49
Jani's Summer Salad, 42
Kerrie Ann's 1000 Island Dressing, 36
La Ratatouille Nicoise, 121
Lemon Celery Soup, 48
Lemon-Dill Turkey Pitas, 113
Lemon Rice, 77
Marinated Carrot Salad, 43
Marinated Carrots, 85
Mexican Eggplant, 118
Mexican Vegetable Lasagna, 106
Mexican Zucchini Bake, 100
Micro Beef Tostada Pie, 99
Mozzarella and Tomato Salad, 45
Old South Jambalaya, 96
Onion Pie, 82
Onion Rings, 10
Pancit Noodles with Vegetables, 91
Pasta Fazool, 96
Potato Leek Soup, 50
Pueblo Wrap, 115
Quick New England Clam Chowder, 50
Quickie Stuffed Peppers, 125
Red and White Salad, 39
Rosemary's Chicken, 90
Salad Dressing, 32
Sausage and Peppers, 95
Savory Herb and Bleu Cheesecake, 14
Scalloped Onions, 11
Shipwreck, 94
Shrimp Mousse, 13
Southern France Green Beans, 80
Southwestern 3 Bean and Corn Salsa, 18
Spaghetti Sauce, 27
Spicy Hot Green Tomato Preserves, 26
Spinach Cheese Pie, 111
Split Pea Soup, 51
Squash Dressing, 36
Squash Supreme, 87
Stephanie's Garden Vegetable Soup, 58
Stuffed Bell Peppers, 112
Stuffed Cabbage Rolls, 116
Stuffed Italian Tomatoes, 78
Stuffed Pumpkin, 105
Stuffed Tomatoes, 122
Stuffed Zucchini, 125
Summer Pasta Salad, 46
Sun Stuffed Peppers, 122
Tomato Soup, 62
Tri-Pasta Salad, 38
Vegetable and Cheese Chowder, 61
Vegetable Antipasto, 81
Vegetable Chili, 59

Vegetable Herb Marinade, 20
Vegetable Medley Soup, 60
Vegetables and Rice, 95
Veggie Pasta Toss, 80
Whole Stuffed Pumpkin with Sausage, 110
Zesty Zucchini Squares, 10
Zucchini and Tomato Casserole, 116
Zucchini Casserole, 107
Zucchini Country Style, 88
Zucchini Crescent Bake, 82
Zucchini Pizza, 119
Zucchini Soup, 51
Zucchini Squash Relish, 28

Onion Pie, 82
Onion Rings, 10
orange
- Chocolate Chip Orange Crunchies, 155
- Cranberry Orange Cake, 143

oregano
- Black Bean Burgers with Banana Ketchup, 120
- Chili-Cheese Chicken Soup with Rice, 53
- Chunky Mushroom Chili, 58
- Eggplant Italiano, 118
- Herbed Shallots in Phyllo Purses, 16
- Italian Salad, 74
- Mexican Vegetable Lasagna, 106
- Mozzarella and Tomato Salad, 45
- Pasta Fazool, 96
- Savory Herb and Bleu Cheesecake, 14
- Southwestern 3 Bean and Corn Salsa, 18
- Spaghetti Sauce, 27
- Stuffed Pumpkin, 105
- Summer Pasta Salad, 46
- Tomatoes Stuffed with Antipasto Salad, 84
- Vegetable Antipasto, 81
- Zucchini Crescent Bake, 82
- Zucchini Pizza, 119

P

pancetta
- Pasta Fazool, 96

Pancit Noodles with Vegetables, 91
Parmesan-Green Peppercorn Dressing, 33
parsley
- Avocado and Tomato Salad with Basil Vinaigrette, 41
- Chicken Piccata, 98
- Garden Delight, 94
- Herb Salt, 33
- Herbed Chicken Breast, 100
- Herbed Shallots in Phyllo Purses, 16
- Italian Salad, 74
- Northport Picante, 22
- Old South Jambalaya, 96
- Parsley Pesto, 25
- Pasta Fazool, 96
- Potato Leek Soup, 50
- Quick New England Clam Chowder, 50
- Savory Herb and Bleu Cheesecake, 14
- Sliced Baked Potatoes, 78
- Southwestern 3 Bean and Corn Salsa, 18
- Split Pea Soup, 51
- Stuffed Italian Tomatoes, 78
- Stuffed Zucchini, 125
- Tabbouleh, 30
- Tomatoes Stuffed with Antipasto Salad, 84
- Vegetable and Cheese Chowder, 61
- White Clam Sauce, 35
- Zesty Zucchini Squares, 10
- Zucchini Crescent Bake, 82
- Zucchini Soup, 51

Parsley Pesto, 25

pasta
    Garden Macaroni Salad, 43
    Garden Minestrone Soup, 56
    Hail Hail for Kale Soup, 54
    Pancit Noodles with Vegetables, 91
    Pasta Fazool, 96
    Shrimp Fettuccine with Sun-Dried Tomatoes, 79
    Summer Pasta Salad, 46
    Tri-Pasta Salad, 38
    Veggie Pasta Toss, 80
Pasta Fazool, 96
peaches
    Peach Custard Pie, 144
Peach Custard Pie, 144
peas
    Chicken À la Tom, 110
    Chicken Pot Pie, 108
    Split Pea Soup, 51
    Stephanie's Garden Vegetable Soup, 58
    Vegetable and Cheese Chowder, 61
peppers
    Black Bean Burgers with Banana Ketchup, 120
    Camille's Eggplant Casserole, 104
    Chicken Breast in Sour Cream, 101
    Chicken Tortilla Soup, 48
    Chili-Cheese Chicken Soup with Rice, 53
    Cody's Soup, 55
    Corned Beef Dip, 18
    Cowboy Salad, 42
    Creole Chicken Pie, 117
    Fiesta Corn Casserole, 124
    Fire-Roasted Tomato Chipotle Salsa, 19
    Frozen Cucumbers, 15
    Garden Delight, 94
    Garden Macaroni Salad, 43
    Gourmet Mint Butter, 27
    Grilled Vegetables and Chicken Sandwich, 103
    Hamburger Pie, 103
    Hot Pepper Butter, 29
    La Ratatouille Nicoise, 121
    Lemon Rice, 77
    Marinated Carrot Salad, 43
    Marinated Carrots, 85
    Mexican Eggplant, 118
    Mexican Vegetable Lasagna, 106
    Mexican Zucchini Bake, 100
    Micro Beef Tostada Pie, 99
    Northport Picante, 22
    Old South Jambalaya, 96
    Pescado Fabiola, 99
    Pueblo Wrap, 115
    Quickie Stuffed Peppers, 125
    Salad Dressing, 32
    Sausage and Peppers, 95
    Southwestern Caesar Salad, 44
    Southwestern 3 Bean and Corn Salsa, 18
    Spaghetti Sauce, 27
    Stuffed Bell Peppers, 112
    Stuffed Pumpkin, 105
    Sun Stuffed Peppers, 122
    Taco Dip, 23
    Tomatoes Stuffed with Antipasto Salad, 84
    Vegetable Chili, 59
    Vegetables and Cheese Chowder, 61
    Veggie Pasta Toss, 80
    Zucchini Country Style, 88
    Zucchini Squash Relish, 28
pepperoncini
    Tomatoes Stuffed with Antipasto Salad, 84
pepperoni
    Caldo Verde, 55
    Veggie Pasta Toss, 80
    Zesty Zucchini Squares, 10

Pescado Fabiola, 99
phyllo dough
    Herbed Shallots in Phyllo Purses, 16
Piccadilly Cafeteria's Carrot Soufflé, 88
Pickled Homegrown Garlic, Beans or Asparagus, 30
pine nuts
    Garden Vegetable Pilaf, 85
    Parsley Pesto, 25
    Stuffed Zucchini, 125
pineapple
    Carrot Cake with Butter Cream Frosting, 145
    Elegant Beet Salad, 38
pinto beans
    Southwestern 3 Bean and Corn Salsa, 18
    Vegetable Chili, 59
pork chops
    Pork Chops with Rhubarb Dressing, 107
Pork Chops with Rhubarb Dressing, 107
potatoes
    Aloo Ghobi, 74
    Caldo Verde, 55
    Cody's Soup, 55
    Cornish Pasties, 105
    Country Goulash, 98
    Garden Delight, 94
    German Potato Salad, 39
    Hamburger Pie, 103
    Italian Salad, 74
    Lemon Celery Soup, 48
    Mashed Potato Cake, 144
    Pescado Fabiola, 99
    Potato Leek Soup, 50
    Potato Puffs, 11
    Pumpkin Brownies, 133
    Quick New England Clam Chowder, 50
    Rosemary's Chicken, 90
    Shipwreck, 94
    Sliced Baked Potatoes, 78
    Stephanie's Garden Vegetable Soup, 58
    Stuffed Bell Peppers, 112
    Vegetable and Cheese Chowder, 61
    Vegetable Medley Soup, 60
Potato Leek Soup, 50
Potato Puffs, 11
proscuitto
    Tomatoes Stuffed with Antipasto Salad, 84
Pueblo Wrap, 115
pumpkin
    Harvest Pumpkin Cobbler, 134
    Mamie Eisenhower's Pumpkin Chiffon Pie, 139
    Pumpkin Brownies, 133
    Pumpkin Cream Cheese Muffins, 140
    Pumpkin Walnut Cheesecake, 151
    Stuffed Pumpkin, 105
    Whole Stuffed Pumpkin with Sausage, 110
Pumpkin Brownies, 133
Pumpkin Cream Cheese Muffins, 140
Pumpkin Walnut Cheesecake, 151

Q
Quick New England Chowder, 50
Quickie Stuffed Peppers, 125

R
radishes
    Garden Macaroni Salad, 43
    Red and White Salad, 39
raisins
    Carrot Cake with Butter Cream Frosting, 145
    Green Tomato Pie, 131
    Irma Jane's Applesauce Cake, 149
    New England Apple Roll, 129
    Stuffed Zucchini, 125

Red and White Salad, 39
Red Apple Cobbler, 130
rhubarb
    Best Rhubarb Shortcake, 152
    Cream Cheese Rhubarb Pie, 135
    Pork Chops with Rhubarb Dressing, 107
    Rhubarb Cake, 153
    Rhubarb Crunch, 146
    Rhubarb Pudding, 141
    Strawberry Rhubarb Muffins, 71
Rhubarb Cake, 153
Rhubarb Crunch, 146
Rhubarb Pudding, 141
rice
    Camille's Eggplant Casserole, 104
    Chicken and Rice Soup, 60
    Chicken Piccata, 98
    Chili-Cheese Chicken Soup with Rice, 53
    Garden Vegetable Pilaf, 85
    Lemon Rice, 77
    Mexican Zucchini Bake, 100
    Old South Jambalaya, 96
    Quickie Stuffed Peppers, 125
    Rice, Cheese and Tomato Casserole, 90
    Shipwreck, 94
    Spinach Cheese Pie, 111
    Stuffed Cabbage Rolls, 116
    Stuffed Pumpkin, 105
    Sun Stuffed Peppers, 122
    Vegetables and Rice, 95
Rice, Cheese and Tomato Casserole, 90
Rose Muffins, 67
rosemary
    Eggplant Italiano, 118
    Herbed Shallots in Phyllo Purses, 16
    Rosemary's Chicken, 90
    Pasta Fazool, 96
    Pork Chops with Rhubarb Dressing, 107
    Savory Herb and Bleu Cheesecake, 14
    Vegetable Herb Marinade, 20
Rosemary's Chicken, 90
roses
    Rose Muffins, 67

S
sage
    Herbed Shallots in Phyllo Purses, 15
    Italy's Peasant-Style Tomato Bread Soup, 49
    Sliced Baked Potatoes, 78
Salad Dressing, 32
sausage
    Cajun Cabbage, 124
    Camille's Eggplant Casserole, 104
    Country Goulash, 98
    Mexican Zucchini Bake, 100
    Old South Jambalaya, 96
    Sausage and Peppers, 95
    Whole Stuffed Pumpkin with Sausage, 110
Sausage and Peppers, 95
Savory Herb and Bleu Cheesecake, 14
scallions
    Michelle's Jam-Packed Meatballs, 126
    Northport Picante, 22
    Stuffed Zucchini, 125
    Tabbouleh, 30
    Tomato Pie, 112
Scalloped Onions, 11
shallots
    Elegant Beet Salad, 38
    Herbed Shallots in Phyllo Purses, 16
Shipwreck, 94
shrimp
    Pancit Noodles with Vegetables, 91

index 159

Shrimp Fettuccine with Sun-Dried Tomatoes, 79
Shrimp Mousse, 13
Shrimp Fettuccine with Sun-Dried Tomatoes, 79
Shrimp Mousse, 13
Sliced Baked Potatoes, 78
Southern France Green Beans, 80
Southwestern Caesar Salad, 44
Southwestern 3 Bean and Corn Salsa, 18
Spaghetti Sauce, 27
Spicy Hot Green Tomato Preserves, 26
spinach
    Ann's Party Spinach, 121
    Lemon Celery Soup, 48
    Mozzarella and Tomato Salad, 45
    Spinach Cheese Pie, 111
    Stuffed Italian Tomatoes, 78
Spinach Cheese Pie, 111
Split Pea Soup, 51
squash
    Green/Yellow Garden Wheel, 104
    Mexican Zucchini Bake, 100
    Squash Dressing, 36
    Squash Pie, 133
    Squash Supreme, 87
    Vegetable Chili, 59
    Winter Squash Bread, 64
    Zucchini Squash Relish, 28
Squash Dressing, 36
Squash Pie, 133
Squash Supreme, 87
Stephanie's Garden Vegetable Soup, 58
strawberries
    Fresh Strawberry Pie, 138
    Jani's Summer Salad, 42
    Strawberry Bread, 70
    Strawberry Pie, 139
    Strawberry Rhubarb Muffins, 71
    Zucchini Strawberry Jam, 27
Strawberry Bread, 70
Strawberry Pie, 139
Strawberry Rhubarb Muffins, 71
Stuffed Bell Peppers, 112
Stuffed Cabbage Rolls, 116
Stuffed Italian Tomatoes, 78
Stuffed Pumpkin, 105
Stuffed Tomatoes, 122
Stuffed Zucchini, 125
Stuffed-Fried Zucchini Blossoms, 15
Summer Pasta Salad, 46
Summer Pasta with Fresh Tomatoes and Herbs, 77
summer savory
    Summer Pasta with Fresh Tomatoes and Herbs, 77
Sun Stuffed Peppers, 122
sunflower seeds
    Sun Stuffed Peppers, 122
    Tuna Delights, 9
sweet potatoes
    Sweet Potato Casserole, 75
Sweet Potato Casserole, 75

T

Tabbouleh, 30
Taco Dip, 23
tarragon
    Chicken Piccata, 98
    Chicken Tarragon, 101
    Green/Yellow Garden Wheel, 104
    Savory Herb and Bleu Cheesecake, 14
thyme
    Black Bean Burgers with Banana Ketchup, 120
    Fiesta Corn Casserole, 124
    Green/Yellow Garden Wheel, 104
    Herb Salt, 33
    Herbed Shallots in Phyllo Purses, 16
    La Ratatouille Nicoise, 121
    Lemon and Thyme Flounder, 108
    Savory Herb and Bleu Cheesecake, 14
    Sliced Baked Potatoes, 78
    Stuffed Cabbage Rolls, 116
    Summer Pasta with Fresh Tomatoes and Herbs, 77
    Tomato Soup, 62
    Vegetable Herb Marinade, 20
    Whole Stuffed Pumpkin with Sausage, 110
tomatoes
    Aloo Ghobi, 74
    Ann's Party Spinach, 121
    Avocado and Tomato Salad with Basil Vinaigrette, 41
    Cajun Cabbage, 124
    Chili-Cheese Chicken Soup with Rice, 53
    Chunky Mushroom Chili, 58
    Cody's Soup, 55
    Cowboy Salad, 42
    Creole Chicken Pie, 117
    Eggplant Italiano, 118
    Fire-Roasted Tomato Chipotle Salsa, 19
    Garden Macaroni Salad, 43
    Garden Minestrone Soup, 56
    Green Tomato Pickles, 26
    Green Tomato Pie, 131
    Hail Hail for Kale Soup, 54
    Hamburger Pie, 103
    Italian Salad, 74
    Italy's Peasant-Style Tomato Bread Soup, 49
    La Ratatouille Nicoise, 121
    Lake Charles Dip, 20
    Mexican Vegetable Lasagna, 106
    Micro Beef Tostada Pie, 99
    Mozzarella and Tomato Salad, 45
    Northport Picante, 22
    Pasta Fazool, 96
    Pescado Fabiola, 99
    Pueblo Wrap, 115
    Rice, Cheese and Tomato Casserole, 90
    Rosemary's Chicken, 90
    Salad Dressing, 32
    Shipwreck, 94
    Shrimp Fettuccine with Sun-Dried Tomatoes, 79
    Southern France Green Beans, 80
    Southwestern 3 Bean and Corn Salsa, 18
    Spaghetti Sauce, 27
    Spicy Hot Green Tomato Preserves, 26
    Stephanie's Garden Vegetable Soup, 58
    Stuffed Bell Peppers, 112
    Stuffed Italian Tomatoes, 78
    Stuffed Pumpkin, 105
    Stuffed Tomatoes, 122
    Stuffed Zucchini, 125
    Summer Pasta Salad, 46
    Summer Pasta with Fresh Tomatoes and Herbs, 77
    Tabbouleh, 30
    Taco Dip, 23
    Tomato Pie, 112
    Tomato Soup, 62
    Tomatoes Stuffed with Antipasto Salad, 84
    Tri-Pasta Salad, 38
    Tuna Delights, 9
    Vegetable Chili, 59
    Vegetable Medley Soup, 60
    Veggie Pasta Toss, 80
    Whole Stuffed Pumpkin with Sausage, 110
    Zucchini and Tomato Casserole, 116
Tomato Pie, 112
Tomato Soup, 62
Tomatoes Stuffed with Antipasto Salad, 84
Tri-Pasta Salad, 38
tuna
    Tuna Delights, 9
Tuna Delights, 9
turkey
    Lemon-Dill Turkey Pitas, 113
    Pueblo Wrap, 115

U

Upside Down Vegetable Dish, 93

V

Vegetable and Cheese Chowder, 61
Vegetable Antipasto, 81
Vegetable Chili, 59
Vegetable Herb Marinade, 20
Vegetable Medley Soup, 60
Vegetables and Rice, 95
Veggie Pasta Toss, 80

W

Walnut Carrot Cake, 146
White Clam Sauce, 35
Whole Stuffed Pumpkin with Sausage, 110
Winter Squash Bread, 64

Z

Zesty Zucchini Squares, 10
Zucchini
    Bread Machine Zucchini Bread, 67
    Cherry Nut Zucchini Bread, 68
    Chicken Tortilla Soup, 48
    Chocolate Zucchini Cake, 136
    Diane Schmitt's Zucchini Pie, 136
    Garden Loaf, 64
    Garden Minestrone Soup, 56
    Green/Yellow Garden Wheel, 104
    Italian Salad, 74
    La Ratatouille Nicoise, 121
    Lemon Zucchini Cookies, 155
    Mini-Chocolate Chip and Coconut Zucchini Loaves, 65
    Mock Crab Cakes, 13
    Stuffed Zucchini, 125
    Stuffed-Fried Zucchini Blossoms, 15
    Vegetable Chili, 59
    Whole Stuffed Pumpkin with Sausage, 110
    Zesty Zucchini Squares, 10
    Zucchini and Clam Casserole, 93
    Zucchini and Tomato Casserole, 116
    Zucchini Apple Bread, 69
    Zucchini Bread, 68
    Zucchini Casserole, 107
    Zucchini Country Style, 88
    Zucchini Crescent Bake, 82
    Zucchini Crisp, 154
    Zucchini Pizza, 119
    Zucchini Soup, 51
    Zucchini Squash Relish, 28
    Zucchini Strawberry Jam, 27
Zucchini and Clam Casserole, 93
Zucchini and Tomato Casserole, 116
Zucchini Apple Bread, 69
Zucchini Bread, 68
Zucchini Casserole, 107
Zucchini Country Style, 88
Zucchini Crescent Bake, 82
Zucchini Crisp, 154
Zucchini Pizza, 119
Zucchini Soup, 51
Zucchini Squash Relish, 28
Zucchini Strawberry Jam, 27